Bright Ideas

INSIGHTS FROM LEGAL
LUMINARIES WORLDWIDE

*26 essays by global legal industry leaders
on where we've been and where we're going*

Bright Ideas

INSIGHTS FROM LEGAL
LUMINARIES WORLDWIDE

---

26 essays by global legal industry leaders
on where we've been and where we're going

EDITED BY E. LEIGH DANCE

Mill City Press, Inc.
212 3rd Avenue North, Suite 290
Minneapolis, MN 55401
612.455.2294
www.millcitypublishing.com

ISBN - 978-1-934937-78-5
ISBN - 1-934937-78-9
LCCN - 2009926255

Cover Design and Typeset by Kristeen Wegner

Printed in the United States of America

This book of essays was created to celebrate
the 15-year anniversary of ELD International,
a management consultancy founded and led by E. Leigh Dance.

Contents

i

Contents

OTHER SIDES:

Foreword

Jan Eijsbouts
Former General Counsel
Akzo Nobel, Amsterdam

It is a great pleasure to introduce Leigh Dance's book on the occasion of the fifteen-year birthday of her global legal services consultancy, ELD International, Inc. Leigh and I have worked together on many projects for the last six years, facilitating practical exchanges and promoting critical thinking among business lawyers globally. We share the same objective: to advance the structures, management and transparency of corporate legal services to meet the needs of the changing world around us.

I have met few individuals that have been as closely involved as Leigh Dance in the many developments in our industry globally— both as they affect corporate legal teams and law firms. Through her consultancy she has contributed significantly to the high quality of international corporate legal advice. The outstanding list of legal luminaries that readily agreed to write essays specifically for this book is the best testimony to Leigh's talents. She helped select and develop the essay topics with each author and was integrally involved in the editing. The result should make both ELD International and the essay contributors very proud.

Landslide Shift in Corporate Legal Advice

The last fifteen years have witnessed a landslide shift in the international legal business profession, including how legal advice is rendered to corporations. The root causes are many: globalization of business, proliferation of regulation, governance demands for stringent risk management and compliance measures in response to scandals, new conflict management techniques, technology advances, and the increasing importance of all of the above in corporate social responsibility and protecting the company's reputation.

My experiences in these fields have led me to three conclusions. First: legal aspects of international business have become so important for achieving a company's objectives that highly experienced, skilled and proactive legal advice is indispensable in day-to-day business management. Second: this legal advice can only be given with a profound knowledge of the business, keen understanding of the global business strategies and policies, and intimate familiarity with the company's culture and code of conduct. In-house counsel are thus best placed to manage the rendering of this advice. Third: inside and outside counsel are natural allies. They need a seamless and committed working relationship to guarantee the timeliness, quality and cost effectiveness of the advice, all of which must come from perfect mutual trust and resolve.

Corporate Law Department as International Law Firm

As a consequence of these conclusions, I see the modern corporate legal department of the transnational company as an international law firm in its own right, with three dimensions: general business lawyers with global responsibility, legal specialists in the core legal fields for the company's operations, and in-house lawyers on the ground in the main jurisdictions where the company conducts its business. International practice groups, knowledge and contract management systems, risk and conflict management systems, management development and career systems, intranets and even legal department business managers are all needed to run such a complicated in-house legal function. Also crucial for this function is a set of law firms with established relationships with the in-house lawyers and a solid understanding of the company's business, strategies, policies and importantly, places where it operates worldwide.

Because of the above shifts, the focal point for corporate legal services management is definitively in-house. This is manifest in the rise of the General Counsel position, and the troublesome trend for regulators to target them in their compliance enforcement actions. It reminds us of the paramount importance of first class ethics and legal compliance systems.

In my former capacities as General Counsel of Akzo Nobel and Co-chair of the IBA Corporate Counsel Forum, I have been able to profit greatly from Leigh's extensive knowledge, her excellent consulting skills, and perhaps above all I've enjoyed her special personal and professional style. I'm honored that she invited me to write this foreword.

To those of you who have read this far, I encourage you to jump in, and profit from the many superb ideas and thought-provoking perspectives advanced in these pages.

Introduction and Acknowledgements

E. Leigh Dance
President, ELD International, Inc.
Water Mill (New York) and Rome

As business professionals zipping around a dynamic world, we are mostly *do-ers*. Our days are loaded with things to do, and our performance is judged according to what we get *done* (it's assumed that it will be done well).* The modern means by which we move across terrain, time zones, cultures— as well as in and out of airplanes, trains and conference rooms—give us precious little time to reflect. Information comes at us fast and furious from every angle, all the time. We are under continuous pressure to deliver.

I started my international consultancy more than 15 years ago, and the independence has allowed me an original lifestyle. But from the work angle, demands on me are the same as on everyone else. It's true that sometimes I do a telecon while picking rosemary at our place in Umbria, or catch up on email from the steps of London's Royal Academy of Art.

But I am also furiously *doing* as I criss-cross the continents. My clients are happy with actions that bring results. Like them, I want to see a big impact. I want to achieve.

With all this focus on *doing*, good old-fashioned *think*ing often gets short shrift. I'm talking about *thinking*, such as when you pause more than three seconds between *receive* and *respond*, or *problem* and *solution*. Like the Zen monks that chop wood and haul water for hours on end as they ponder life's big questions. Thinking is that delightfully disciplined experience of settling on something only after gathering and mulling around a lot of complex ideas and information.

Critical Thinking, Now More than Ever

Though we rightly reward the *doing*, we also know that challenges in the global legal arena require critical *thinking*. Of course you need leadership and talent, but it's often the thinking that enables you to attract and retain that leadership and talent. It's the concepts that often bring competitive differentiation. It's thinking through the right approach that can make the execution brilliantly successful. We can keep on aggressively *doing* until the pedals fall off our treadmills (and maybe no one will notice we've been going in circles). What truly propels us forward are the great ideas that are implemented, adjusted and perfected.

Fueled by the desire to go places in this world, and raised with a conviction (from my country's founding fathers) that great ideas and good people can take us far, I decided to ask a number of colleagues to share their thinking. In autumn 2008, on the occasion of my consultancy's 15th birthday, I invited many individuals who have been important to me and my consultancy. I asked them to write on one of a selection of topics that intrigued me, or come up with their own, and amazingly, almost everyone accepted. In some cases I conducted interviews and wrote a first draft. Most people wrote their own. Except for a short piece from last year's *FT*, I focused on editing and did not contribute an essay (you can find my articles at www.eldinternational.com).

The people that wrote the essays in this book are very successful. They are quintessential *do*-ers on a global scale and I admire them tremendously. As you'll see from the Author Profiles following the essays, they come from lots of countries, have been lots of places, and are generous with what they know. In addition to their impressive backgrounds and experience, they also have some really bright ideas.

Global Legal Industry Today Faces Multi-dimensional Issues

Given my traipsing around the world for 25 years or so, I often spot cross-border trends and changes. The last 18 months have been amazingly full of them, which is why I proclaim that the global legal industry today is not at a crossroads. It's something far more three-dimensional than that, and the multiple layers demand more rigorous thinking, assembling or restructuring, and integrating.

Whether running a global law firm or corporate law department, choices must be made about a very wide range of issues. As you take action and your organization changes, a share of chaos may be inevitable. It will settle. If people are consistently clear about where they are going and the how and why, they will usually get there. These ideas should help you along the way.

A word about order: after the Table of Contents, there is no intended sequence of essays. They are roughly divided by executives in corporate law departments (in alpha order by author's name), executives in law firms, and other commentators.

Thank You

I am profoundly grateful to everyone who took their valuable time to contribute. It has been so rewarding to work with each of you on your essay. Thank you to the clients who have partnered with me on such excellent projects over the last 15 years. To Gail Jaffa and Marilyn Hoyle who worked with ELD International in London and Rome: a debt of gratitude for your good work and your camaraderie. Thank you to my six consulting allies, who I couldn't do without. Special thanks go to Bruno Cova of Paul Hastings for initially and consistently encouraging me on the book concept, to Jay Sauerbrei of Accenture for his helpful tips and enthusiasm, and to Jan Eijsbouts for his foreword.

As a gesture of my appreciation to all of you, profits from sales of this book will go to the good work of Advocates for International Development (www.A4ID.org), a non-profit organization and international pro-bono broker (see Chapter 13).

Turning to two very special people with lots of their own bright ideas, I want to thank my husband Aldo Mazzoni and my daughter Anna Livia, for enduring my demanding career and still welcoming me warmly when I come home.

Finally, I must acknowledge the fine inside and outside counsel and other legal industry professionals that I have the good fortune to meet with in so many cities around the world. You continually amaze me with your lucid insights and your good humor. On those frequent occasions when I feel perplexed by this complex world, you give me wise, clever and creative approaches to address issues and seize opportunities. I hope you enjoy the book. Let me know what you think.

E. Leigh Dance

---

*Credit goes to Mike O'Neill for this concept, found in Chapter 5 entitled *Fit for Global*.

1.
Living Through a Corporate Crisis and Preparing for What Might Come Next

Peter J. Beshar
Executive VP and General Counsel
Marsh & McLennan Companies, New York

What happened to Lehman Brothers? And to Bear Stearns? I'm not sure that even the people at Lehman Brothers or Bear Stearns could tell you. Was it a run on the bank? Was it activity by shorts? The only certainty is that what were once the fourth and fifth largest investment banks in the US are no longer. And that it happened with breathtaking speed—by most accounts, in 72 hours.

A few years ago, Marsh & McLennan (MMC) came very close to suffering the fate of Lehman Brothers and Bear Stearns. Having served as the head of Legal for MMC through that crisis, I will share with you what we did during our crisis and some insights I've gained along the way.

Background

In late 2004, then New York Attorney General Eliot Spitzer dropped a bomb on Marsh. The AG's office filed a complaint charging Marsh with illegal bid rigging. Later that morning, two AIG employees pleaded guilty

1

to conspiring with Marsh to rig bids. At a press conference announcing the charges, Spitzer stated that he would not negotiate with MMC's senior management and would "very possibly" indict Marsh. The reaction was swift and severe. Within minutes, MMC's stock price plummeted, erasing billions in market capitalization. The rating agencies downgraded MMC's A+ credit rating by four notches. With $2 billion of commercial paper coming due from the Kroll acquisition, the Company was effectively shut off from the public debt markets or additional bank financing.

The Company was thrown into turmoil. The New York Insurance Department threatened to revoke Marsh's license to do business. In the corporate counsel's office, you can imagine the bedlam: more than 60 Federal and State regulators filed subpoenas demanding information —22 Attorneys General, 38 insurance commissioners, and an alphabet soup of Federal agencies, the SEC, DOL, PBGC, GSA. Every form of civil litigation that exists in America—securities, policyholders, ERISA, derivative—was filed within a matter of days if not hours.

Clients were outraged and demanded to know if any of their hundreds of thousands of placements were impacted. Employees were devastated—concerned of course about their jobs, their stock plans, their pensions—but also dismayed that one of the greatest collection of brands in the world could be damaged so swiftly and severely. In sum, in a matter of hours, the viability of a Fortune 200 company with a proud 130-year history, $12BN in revenue and 60,000 employees, was in doubt. The question was: Can a "people" business in fact withstand a corporate indictment?

Response and Reaction

If you haven't been inside one of these "hurricanes," it is hard to fathom the pace and dynamic nature of the process. The first question: who was in charge to lead us through the crisis? Chain of command is critical in a crisis but Spitzer had, in effect, decapitated the organization. He said that he would not negotiate with Jeff Greenberg, the then-CEO of MMC. It then fell to Mike Cherkasky, who had run Kroll, to try to stave off a criminal indictment of the corporation. Arthur Andersen was still fresh in people's minds.

At this point in the crisis, I was a happy person. I was a litigation partner at Gibson, Dunn & Crutcher. A few days later, I was contacted about becoming the General Counsel at MMC. I was given 48 hours to accept and seven days to start, a clear sign of what was to come.

At 8:00 a.m. on my first day on the job, I called Spitzer. I went downtown that day and had an exceedingly pleasant exchange. It would be the last time. The negotiations with Spitzer and his staff were brutal, and both physically and mentally exhausting. Having been contacted by literally scores of other law enforcement authorities and regulators, we wanted a global deal. The Attorney General's office said no; you will do a deal with us or not at all. In response, we insisted on two provisions; first, any payment made by Marsh could not be a fine or a penalty. Monies couldn't be seen as going into the coffers of New York State. It also had the important effect of making the payment tax deductible. Second, we needed restitution to be made available to our clients across the country—not simply to policyholders in New York.

The next few days were a rollercoaster. On Friday night, January 28, the negotiations collapsed. At 10:00 p.m. on Saturday night, there was a flurry of calls. They were willing to do a deal if it was concluded by Sunday evening. A frantic day of negotiations on Sunday ended at midnight. Within minutes of announcing the settlement on Monday morning, we reached out to other regulators. Some hung up on us. If all you knew about Marsh & McLennan was what you read in the headlines, it is hardly surprising that you would take an exceedingly dim view of the company. Visiting state capitols around the country, we tried to first, humanize the corporation that had been demonized, second, explain the almost unprecedented remedial steps that we had taken, and third, make clear that there were tens of thousands of honorable professionals who made up the Marsh & McLennan Companies.

Communications

Inside and outside the company, advisors counseled against engaging our clients. They believed it would only lead to heartache. They pleaded "Let them cool down and then try to engage them." We rejected this approach for fear that, if we waited, there might not be any clients left. We sent a letter to all clients and conducted five separate "open microphone" calls with clients. On the first call, 9,000 lines were used. We knew the plaintiffs' lawyers were on the calls. On one call, a client asked if they could come in to our offices and inspect their files. I had signaled – no. The CEO, of course, responded "absolutely." Hundreds if not thousands of clients did just that.

In May 2005 we sent notices to more than 100,000 clients describing our restitution fund and each client's allocated share. To receive a distribution, each client had to sign a release. We intentionally did not hawk or advocate for a settlement. We left the choice to the client, betting over the response rate. Ultimately, over 90 percent of the fund was claimed. That response rate has been important to our subsequent dialog with regulators outside New York. In most states, 48 or 49 of Marsh's top 50 customers chose to opt into the settlement. In addition, the releases were a critical element to our defense in the policyholder class actions.

During a crisis, it is tempting to focus less energy internally. But this Company is made up of talented people who have served us very well. They made Marsh the #1 insurance broker, Mercer the #1 benefits consultant, Kroll the #1 risk consultant and Guy Carpenter the #1 reinsurance broker. We're a service company, and that means that our assets get on the elevator every night and need a reason to come back in the morning. We tried to communicate continuously even though uncomfortable questions were asked. How many people were engaged in the alleged bid rigging? Has all the misconduct been identified? We didn't have hard answers to every question but we kept the dialog open. We conducted seven all-colleague conference calls in three months. We also needed our employees to work with us on solving the problem. Part of our agreement with Spitzer was a comprehensive compliance program worldwide, and so we had to quickly implement extensive training and controls in a matter of months.

Recommendations:

So what can we take away from all this? Scarred by our crisis at Marsh & McLennan, here are seven, humble recommendations for avoiding or managing a crisis and preparing for what's next:

1) Stay in touch with your stakeholders. Nobody has a monopoly on wisdom. If there are good, even if unconventional, ideas out there, listen to them.

2) Conduct a serious risk assessment. Goldman Sachs and BlackRock provided textbook examples of how to anticipate the sub-prime crisis and hedge, or even profit from, their positions. Others provide textbook examples of what not to do. What is your Achilles heel?

3) After you have done your risk assessment, throw it out the window for a moment and try to prepare for the unpredictable.

4) Remember that these are not just exercises for senior management. Senior management is sometimes part of the problem. Thus, the board needs to be involved as well. If a vacuum is created, the board can fill it.

5) Be decisive. This is particularly hard for lawyers, since we always want more information to make a more informed decision. In a crisis, you don't have that luxury. You need to make decisions based on the best available information and then don't look back by second guessing yourself.

6) Be positive. In any crisis, people are shell shocked. That was particularly so at Marsh because the workforce had been through a lot: September 11th when Marsh lost 300 colleagues, Putnam market timing and Marsh bid rigging. In that environment, you need to tell people that *"we are going to get through this."* Our managers needed to hear it, my legal team needed to hear it, and thousands of employees all over the world deserved to hear it. Then repeat it – "we *are going to get through this."*

7) Finally, whatever the crisis, keep in mind Winston Churchill's advice—"when you are going through hell, by all means keep going." ●

2.

1° Law™: Building a Better Legal Service Delivery System

Jeffrey Carr
General Counsel
FMC Technologies, Houston

The FMC Technologies legal team constantly tries to find new and better ways to deliver legal services to our customers—the individual business units at our global $4 billion publicly-traded, NYSE listed company. We always try to align our legal services with business objectives, looking to increase value more than just reducing costs. The environment, in which we work, is constantly changing and expanding in geography and complexity, which means we must constantly re-evaluate the way we work. The team focuses on three core functions:

1) Acting as the trusted strategic advisor to the business,
2) Managing risks and protecting assets while maintaining the company's ethical compass, and
3) Delivering cost-effective legal services appropriate to the business.

While our business revenues have nearly doubled since 2001, even though outside legal hourly rates have increased an average of nearly 10% each year, we have been able to keep total legal costs essentially flat. We've also won more cases, reduced case cycle time, reduced total dispute resolution costs and IP costs, and reduced legal spending as a percentage of company revenue. Through our 1° LAW ™ program, we've demonstrated the value the legal team brings to our internal business clients. Overall, our new approach helped us change the way legal services are delivered globally, to provide better and more cost effective results. Equally important, the 1° LAW™ program also aligns our outside counsel with the values of FMC promising a win-win relationship through the adoption of similar approaches and disciplines.

In developing 1° LAW™, we had to question the conventional wisdom of traditional legal services because those methods simply don't work efficiently. We needed to find a way to enable all players to work together and to align our interests, which meant creating a platform and an alternative fee system to be used everywhere.

Some tools had to be invented, while others required adapting off-the-shelf tools and systems to our unusual focus. As more fully explained below, working as a team, and with a focus on continuous improvement, we turned upside down some disciplines traditionally not applied to law, and adapted and embraced them wholeheartedly.

How Does Our Approach Work?

1° LAW™ is a holistic approach in which internal and external lawyers, paraprofessionals, staff and preferred service providers work together enabled by technology to leverage systems, knowledge and human resources to deliver legal services to the corporate customer.

Besides our determination to make it work, the backbone of the system is two-fold:

> 1) an integrated and legal team management system (Serengeti Tracker);
> 2) our homegrown performance-based pay alternative billing system known as ACES™ (Alliance Counsel Engagement System).

These 2 elements gave rise to a series of "principles, rules and tools" that we constantly revalidate and hone to ensure that we are always focused on value and improvements.

Legal Management System

When first forming the FMC Technologies legal team, we found that several disparate and inconsistent tools were used to manage our legal services delivery. The tools included databases (maintained either inside the company or by service providers), spreadsheets or lists (kept in file folders or on yellow pads), and in some cases there were no tools or records. We decided to integrate as many aspects of legal team back office management as possible in order to:

- reduce redundancy
- encourage collaboration
- streamline reporting
- facilitate communication with our internal clients and outside counsel.

We determined that we needed to use an ASP-based software platform that worked outside our internal firewalls. After an examination and review of offerings, we found that Serengeti Tracker best served those needs. And perhaps more important, the Serengeti team responded to the needs of customers like us for enhanced functionality and interoperability.

Performance-Based Pay (The ACES™ Model)

The FMC Technologies Legal team invented the ACES™ program because of the lack of workable and effective fee structures and the resistance of both in-house counsel and law firms to adopt some form of value-based billing. The underlying principles of this alternative fee model are to achieve service relationships based on partnering and sharing of risks and rewards.

Traditionally, the law firm business model is designed to make more money by billing more hours. ACES™ links pay to performance by placing a portion of fees at risk and paying bonuses for efficiency and results.

This enables law firms to make more money per hour while having FMC Technologies buy fewer hours. In other words, the FMC Technologies ACES™ model increases both the firm's per hour profitability and frees up their time to sell to another customer—permitting both top line and margin growth. FMC Technologies' objective is not buying hours but obtaining quality legal services efficiently.

ACES LT™ is our standard model based on a "report card" where law firms receive between 80% and 120% of their invoice. Using an evaluation matrix integrated with the law department's matter management system, law firms are rated on their performance in key metrics that track the law department's core values: Responsiveness; Goals Achievement/ Effectiveness; Knowledge; Predictive Accuracy; and Efficiency. Depending upon performance, law firms may receive zero to 200% of the at-risk fees (i.e., 80%-120% of the firm's invoice). This model can be used for any type of engagement—fixed fee, hourly, retainer, etc.

The more complex ACES™ model is used for outside litigation services. While conceptually similar to ACES LT ™, the litigation model focuses on expeditious resolution to avoid the big ticket expenditures of discovery and trial. It requires that law firms provide an initial assessment of the case with defined objectives, target budgets by phase, work plans, and success estimates. As with ACES LT™ a portion of the billed amount is retained in "at risk." The amount ultimately paid depends upon efficiency, effectiveness and predictive accuracy. A firm could theoretically recover it's at-risk amount plus nearly 300%.

Overall, the ACES™ Model works incredibly well. It pays law firms for success, rewards efficiency, and aligns interests because law firms are focused on success and total disposition costs. At the end of the day, we pay less overall, and the firm realizes more profit per hour. In addition, we have freed up the firm's inventory of hours to sell to others. I call that mutually beneficial leverage!

With these two core systems at the center, 1° Law™ emphasizes four key management competencies:

• **Financial/Administrative Management:** Each law firm agrees to our "Covenant with Counsel" that sets forth our concepts governing the relationship and states each party's commitment to the other philosophically, culturally, promotionally and symbiotically. Each firm has one engagement letter posted to its firm profile that serves as the master services agreement between the company and the firm. "Work orders" for individual matters open a new matter and grant the external firm access to it, thus eliminating repetitive engagement letters and confusion between multi-office firms. Engagements are always based on one of the ACES™ models. External counsel interact with the company through the Tracker™ system. Invoices are submitted and approved electronically through this platform eliminating paper and reducing process. Most payments are made through a VISA purchasing card facility with a 4 to 15 day processing time. Budgets at the matter and annual level are created and administered through the Serengeti system. We thus have metrics and historic data for benchmarking, performance review and continuous improvement. It has been incorporated into our SOX section 404 control for contingent liabilities.

• **Matter Management:** All Legal Team members use the Tracker™ matter management system. Lawyers (both internal and external) are required to input and update all matters in the system. It includes all litigation, IP and general matters and may be sorted to provide current and historic data. The General Counsel has direct, real-time access to all matters in the system, and other lawyers have access to matters for their specific business units and other matters within their specialty area. This information platform and collaborative approach eliminates overlap, with lawyers writing separate reports and/or scheduling meetings to discuss case status. Key internal consumers of legal services such as business managers and controllers have access to their matters as well. Since all external matters have budgets and ACES™-based performance-based pay attributes, the information available to all constituents—clients, management, internal and external lawyers are transparent. Since all matters, are integrated into Tracker™ we foster efficiency, consistency, collaboration and leveraging of information.

• **Relationship Management:** We think about two sets of relationships: with our business customers and with our external counsel. We want to understand business priorities and strategies and align law department activities with them. We also want to communicate with and manage external counsel to encourage efficiency and cost-effectiveness while enabling them to be profitable. Tracker™ provides the platform. It permits reporting and flexible work teams by business unit or subject matter area and therefore serves as a work flow process portal. The ACES™ program links compensation to performance. All matters require an evaluation by outside counsel at least once each year or at the end of the matter, whichever is shorter. These evaluations form the basis for payments of 'at risk' amounts and bonuses under ACES™. They also provide a framework for attorney feedback meetings to calibrate service with expectations. Finally, the system helps us prepare briefing materials for directors and board committees more efficiently than traditional hard-copy board books or new wave, single-purpose internet services.

• **Asset/Risk Management:** When we speak of asset management, we mean physical, IP, financial assets—and perhaps most importantly, knowledge management. For the legal team, asset management involves the leveraging of knowledge and prior work product to protect assets and mitigate risk. In our view, risk management requires a "holistic" approach to legal services, with an overall goal of avoiding disputes and compliance problems. We want fewer disputes with suppliers, providers, customers, and regulators around the world. Litigation is an irritant and takes business people's focus away from core responsibilities. Making new law and trying cases should never be core competencies of FMC Technologies.

We focus on contract risk, operational risk, compliance risk and dispute risk. The 1 LAW™ approach has three components to help manage risk: (1) conflict avoidance through compliance training, better contracting practices, design review, human factor analysis, IP management, and relationship tools; (2) rapid and efficient conflict management and dispute resolution; and (3) after-action reviews to close out transactions, litigation, and administrative matters in order to determine improvements needed and ways to avoid the situation in the first place. This last element (3) closes the circle with the first (1)—using situations and processes to avoid repeating the past. Web-based and other training platforms extend the reach of the legal team while ACES™ provides the economic levers for efficient and successful dispute resolution.

Standard form discipline as well as contract and document assembly programs provide consistency in forms. It also empowers our customers and frees lawyers' time to be counselors. Decision tree software and early case assessment disciplines enforced through Tracker™ supports risk recognition and management. The system also enhances US FASB and SOX accounting compliance and ensures after-action review so that lessons can be captured. Ultimately, this supports our core value of sustainable continuous improvement in business performance.

Conclusion

The 1° Law™ program enables us to achieve our goals of added value fit for our times, through the effective use of technology. For us, it's been revolutionary, and our next step is to build the knowledge management infrastructure to support it. Case cycle time has been reduced, disputes resolved below expected value, law firm evaluations improved, customer service enhanced, and expenditures are flat lines in absolute terms and declining in relative terms. It's helping us to get where we continually strive to go: a seamless and cost-effective integration between the legal team (internal and external) and the business function in our global company. ●

3.
Building and Motivating a High-Performing Global Legal Team

Tim S. Glassett
former General Counsel
Hilton Hotels Corporation, Beverly Hills, CA

It's not easy to build and motivate a legal team that works across an entire country. But for leaders of global legal teams, one country feels like a breeze. Challenges include geography, language, culture, time zones, local laws and customs, and disparate professional education approaches, just to name a few. High performance for the global legal team requires deliberate strategy and regular management attention. The principles in this article come from my learning as a leader of a global legal team and from other global law department leaders. The principles intend to help global law department leaders build a winning team that delivers not just for the business but also to each member's personal and professional satisfaction.

Imagine having a global legal team that thinks like you do. It juggles many projects. It gets results. It gets along with others. It knows its stuff, and willingly shares knowledge and information. It is appreciated by its clients. It enjoys coming to work every day! That can be your legal team, but there are some rules to follow.

In order for the team to really perform, your global legal department must be free of common road blocks to success. Among other things, the leader of the global team must:

- Ensure that lawyers in the department are fairly compensated based on local standards;
- Encourage a work/life balance to cultivate a positive workplace
- Minimize each lawyer's administrative burdens; and
- Take time to visit one-on-one with each lawyer periodically

Build the Right Skills

The first building block of an effective global in-house team is quality talent, with the requisite in-house competencies for your company. Quality talent will not guarantee success, but a significant lack of the right talent may doom a team to mediocrity. Most leaders do not have the opportunity to personally hire every member of the global legal team—they usually inherit many. Early triage to identify the strongest and weakest team members will lay an effective foundation. Weak team members should be given a reasonable opportunity to develop the skills necessary to overcome their weaknesses, but should be given a short leash.

Give People the Work They Like Best

More than anything else, a win-win environment in the global legal team will flow from managing the in-house workload so that every in-house lawyer has an opportunity to do what they are best at and what they enjoy most. Unfortunately most legal managers approach workload in the opposite direction: they determine what needs doing, and then assign the workload accordingly. The result is that many in-house lawyers end up with too much work for which they have little interest.

Lawyers do their best work when doing what they enjoy most. Fortunately, most in-house law departments have more work than they can possibly handle. Recent global benchmarking studies suggest that over half (measured by volume, not cost) of all legal work of the average in-house law department is sent outside. This staffing mix of inside and outside resource yields a great opportunity for law department leaders. Ask your inside lawyers what they enjoy working on, and send the unloved work to outside lawyers. Challenges of geography and expertise will intervene to make this a demanding exercise, but there will be some movement, and that movement will be a strong motivator.

Keep the Structure Flat and Provide a Career Path

The best global legal teams are structured relatively flat. Lawyers are not always the best managers, and their training is generally focused on practicing law. A flat organization lets the lawyers do more of what their training has prepared them for. The one downside to a flat organization is the occasional lack of an apparent career path. Therefore, a good flat legal team will also have an established career path that rewards what it needs most: expertise and responsibility.

For the effective global team, it is not enough to have good lawyers who are hard working or highly productive. They must also have the commonly called "soft skills." They must work collaboratively and often remotely. They should deliberately develop competencies for the global business arena. Soft skills most needed are not taught in law school; subjects like "Dealing with Ambiguity," "Conflict Management" or "Customer Focus." Many good resources are available, such as those published by Lominger (www.lominger.com).

Communicate...but How?

Effective communication is perhaps the most daunting challenge of a global legal team, yet it's a crucial element for success. Without regular and effective "downward communication," your team will become fragmented as individuals wander away from the team strategy towards their own best guesses. Without regular and effective "upward communication" you will not be able to guide the global team.

The basic default communication media for global legal teams are email, telephone, video conference and face-to-face meetings. Email has the luxury of transcending time zones, but as many of us know, it is highly inefficient and ineffective. It can work for "one to few" communications on simple issues that do not have cultural nuances or require collaboration, but that is its limit. Act affirmatively to limit the sanctioned use of email in global communications.

Telephone is more effective than email, but suffers from world time zone logistics and becomes ineffective for collaboration when the participants on a call exceed 8-10. Video conference is slightly better than telephone, but has the same limits. One way to mitigate time zone challenges for telephone and video conferences is to rotate scheduled times and record all meetings (subject to local legal requirements) so the off-cycle participants have an opportunity to catch up.

Face-to-face meetings are the most effective communication method, but are also the least efficient and not often an option for the global legal team. Face-to-face meetings are essential, however, and should be held at least every 18 months. In addition to encouraging spontaneous communication and bonding, face-to-face meetings are the best way to set and reinforce global law department strategy. The whole team thus takes part in developing the strategy, they "buy in," and that strengthens the win-win environment.

At Hilton, I or another member of the law department executive management team personally visited our locations with lawyers at least once every 3 months (or had the lawyers visit headquarters). I spoke to each of my direct reports by phone at least biweekly. When we got together for legal team retreats, we invested many hours to organize the agenda and activities, and to otherwise get input so that we would have the best possible communication at our gathering. We organized cross-border sub-teams prior to the retreat, who met by phone and by email to discuss issues and develop presentations before we all met under one roof. There is no doubt that team performance improves with the frequency of these human communications.

An effective communications approach uses all means available, and optimizes the use of each.

Collaborative Communications Tools

Many collaborative communication tools are now available and really help with foundational communication. One example is Microsoft's Sharepoint (a free add-on to Microsoft Windows Server). It is a browser-based collaboration tool and document-management platform, and in conjunction with a global legal team's intranet, can be used to host shared workspaces and documents, as well as wikis and blogs. The shared documents storage function of Sharepoint is not as powerful as professional document management software, but it is useful for high level knowledge management (brief banks, form files, etc.).

The most powerful informational tool for a global legal team, however, is web-based shared workspaces.

The reason the web based shared workspaces can be so powerful is that they transcend time zones in a "many to many" communications exchange. Shared workspaces are the ideal platform for an optimal 360 degree global legal department management information system (MIS). Using MS Sharepoint "Lists," each of the legal department sub units (whether a practice or region) has a "View" (their own customized page) that they populate at least weekly by each lawyer with brief descriptions of key information (e.g., top 3 developments, top 3 unfavorable developments, all new matters). Users can view only the Highlights if they choose. That way, all lawyers worldwide have a consistent, quick and easy way and frequently receive high level global information. If they want more detailed information, they can go to each of the subunit views. Sharepoint also includes some limited "push" communication tools.

Delegating Authority to Make Decisions

A high-performing global legal team has the real authority to make decisions in real time. If each lawyer must get supervisor approval for routine decisions, they won't develop the confidence to make the legal risk/ business reward judgment calls. Those calls are what make the in-house experience exciting and rewarding. Your global legal team needs limits, of course, but set their authority levels at least equal with the authority levels of the internal clients they support.

There are some limits that require special policies, such as decisions where professional ethical rules are implicated or decisions that impact more than one major client area. Clear internal policies should be set for these limits.

Achieving effective internal communication as discussed above is essential to delegating. Leaders need information to be able to coach on decisions to be made and to prevent internally conflicting advice. When your team makes judgment calls, be supportive. Let them make mistakes without undue consequence, as long as they are willing to listen and to be coached.

Conclusion

These principles are designed to work in an environment where all your lawyers are focused on addressing the legal issues of the day, rather than implementing strategy. Each step includes win-win factors that will keep individual players engaged and encouraged to perform. Each step has something that benefits the individuals who make up the bigger team.

Those steps should lead you to a global legal team that is happy with their work and gets great results. ●

4.
The Regulatory Pendulum Worldwide: Where are we Headed?

Fadi Hammadeh
General Counsel
Dubai Properties Group, Dubai

The world has witnessed many financial crises in the last century, from the Panic of 1907 and the Great Depression of 1929 to the Asian Monetary Crises and the Dotcom Bubble. All these crises have heavily influenced the manner in which we structure our financial institutions, manage our economies and decide on the nature and extent of our regulatory texture.

The Credit Crisis

Whilst the current financial turmoil shares many factors with the previous global crises, it is also unique for several reasons:

- The unprecedented level of globalization of goods and services has meant that financial instruments, including toxic products and junk bonds that are issued in one part of the world, can instantaneously be marketed and sold to consumers all over the globe.

• The interdependence of financial institutions worldwide, in terms of borrowing and extending credit, has meant that if one institution suffers from liquidity problems, there is a ripple effect to the other institutions. The dramatic consumer spending habits that have evolved in the developed world due to easy money floating in the economy (note that the total global equity markets stood at $60 trillion before the crisis, while the total derivatives stood at $385 trillion!).

• The spread of the internet as a global means of marketing and communication influencing the consumption habits of consumers and the way they react to financial crisis. Aggravated agency problems between corporate managers and shareholders where one has grown weary and suspicious of the other, as well as the failure of current corporate governance models to ensure transparency of information and mitigate against conflicts of interest within corporations.

• Increased tension in corporate objectives: between short and long term corporate performance and shareholders vs. stakeholders value maximization.

• Massive bailouts of their national financial institutions by worldwide governments and the extension of the "too big to fall" doctrine. This has cast considerable doubt amongst investors in the theories of efficient markets.

• Incremental deregulation trends and the inability of existing regulations to keep pace with the rapid evolution of diverse and complicated financial instruments and derivatives.

Challenges

Global financial markets shrunk by more than $25 trillion in September 2008 and oil prices plummeted to $50 per barrel a month later from their previous highs of $140 per barrel. The events beg the question: how and to what extent do we need to redesign our regulatory approach in order to help to: (i) restore investors' confidence in the markets and financial institutions to avoid moving from a global recession into a global depression? And (ii) alter the architecture of the financial markets and banking systems so as to avert similar crises in the future?

I have always found it interesting that in times of economic expansion, regulations are often criticized for stifling the entrepreneurial spirit of those who take advantage of the boom. Much effort, money and lobbying is invested to ensure that liberal risk-taking values are kept safe from the rigid arm of the regulators. However, when recession looms on the horizon, the legislator is often blamed for having been too "laid back" and reactive.

A balance therefore needs to be struck. We need to ensure that there are enough adequate regulations in place to protect the general masses from corporate greed, whilst at the same time keeping those regulations flexible and adaptable enough to allow for the individual innovative spirit that has allowed our societies to evolve since the industrial revolution.

Where are we headed?

In order to restore confidence in the market system, the global pendulum should be swinging strongly towards regulatory reforms. In my view, these reforms should aim to achieve the following:

1. The creation of a global supervisory & regulatory body which is capable of acting promptly and efficiently to counter early warning signs of global financial distress. Part of its immediate mandate should be to:
   a) seek an international consensus on liquidity standards for banks and oversee the global protection of bank deposits;
   b) reform the International Monetary Fund and World Bank to ensure that they are tools for long-term economic stability and not just short-term political agendas;
   c) reform credit-rating agencies to avoid conflicts of interest and to annex such agencies, in order to ensure independent and unbiased credit ratings;
   d) reform accounting firms to ensure independent audits and the creation of corporate whistle-blowing protection programs;

e) regulate the operation of hedge funds; and

f) regulate short-selling.

2. The introduction of reforms to the ownership structure and operations of the global banking industry, an industry too important to be left entirely to the whims of the private sector. Legislation will need to be passed to ensure that:

a) governments are afforded a minimum ownership of major banks and their representatives allowed non-executive membership of the boards of directors of such banks;

b) there are higher controls over adequacy of capitalization, lending strategies and the risk-taking approach;

c) banks and financial institutions are only permitted to securitize asset- backed mortgages bearing high ratings. Junk bonds may still be traded, subject to a proper explanation of the associated risks of default conveyed to, understood and agreed by retail buyers in writing.

3. A mandatory move away from shareholders' value maximization towards stakeholders' value maximization as a corporate objective. As the role of the welfare state continues to shrink, corporations are a key element of social stability and thus cannot be allowed to continue to uphold purely capitalistic objectives without proper checks and balances. Corporations cannot ignore the important role they need to play in terms of promoting employees' welfare and market stability when a large portion of their shares continue to be held by pension funds and retail investors.

4. Restructuring of the salary and bonus systems of corporate executives to ensure they are reflective of their corporations' long term real growth rather than short term profitability.

5. Requirements that large corporations maintain viable risk management measures and early fraud detection systems.

6. The development of special penal codes for corporate crimes and

the promotion of strict regulatory enforcement measures to ensure that illegal corporate behavior is promptly sanctioned whilst ethical behavior is adequately rewarded.

7. The compilation of a uniform Corporate Governance model to be made compulsory for all listed corporations around the world. One of the objectives of such initiative will be to ensure that corporate growth and longevity becomes a function of success on equal par with profitability.

The Way Forward

Sometimes we need a crisis to change the status quo. Capitalism and free market concepts in their conventional sense are at a crossroads. The economic theories which are based on *laissez-faire* principles of classical liberalism have strongly advocated free market economies and have criticized government regulatory policies on the basis of market efficiency and rationality. The current financial crisis is inviting us all to reconsider.

Emerging areas of social science such as behavioral finance and the psychology of market panic suggest that markets cannot be as rational as their players are inherently irrational. This can be observed in the US sub-prime crisis which has evolved from a national real estate mortgage crisis into a global credit and financial one, causing loss of market value on an unprecedented global level. Deregulated markets lead to exaggerated risk taking and unrealistic levels of leverage and this in turn can lead to the type of recessionary crises that we are witnessing today. This vicious cycle will need to be broken for the sake of social stability.

The question ought not to be whether there should be more or less regulation. The question should be: how swiftly can we introduce better regulations that stimulate competition and reward entrepreneurial spirit whilst at the same time protecting the many from the greed of the few? ●

5.
Fit for Global: Operating Tenets for the General Counsel

Michael O'Neill
Senior VP and General Counsel
Lenovo Corp, Washington DC

In between the rush and flow of working as General Counsel of Lenovo, a global computer company with heritage in both the US (IBM PC) and China (Legend Computers) and operations worldwide, I've realized that there are some basic principles that guide me in my work. I'll call these Tenets — some of them I've learned on the way and some of them I keep learning every day. Let me share those at the top of my list.

We don't get paid for what we DO—we get paid for what we get DONE

I think this is the single most important rule for success in an in-house role. In my business we often talk in terms of "DONE?" "NOT DONE?" This is the ultimate short summary status for my business people. It's often all my business client has time or inclination for. It's a hard discipline for our function and undermined by our legal education. The nature of legal training is fraught with nuanced facts and precedent applied and analyzed to a legal conclusion. We sometimes preamble and then caveat in the same mouthful. It's no surprise that our outside service providers are mostly programmed to bill by the hour and not the results. But adhering to this Tenet is many times what makes the difference between business partnering (what my clients want) and functional support (the last phylogeny of legal engagement). If I had a mantra for in-house counsel this would be it.

Get an Understanding—Set the Parameters

One of the key things you learn as you move up the organizational ladder is the importance of understanding the drivers of the situation and the players involved, before jumping into the work of resolution. You rarely have the luxury of time, so you need to fast forward that understanding and establish the parameters of the "solution set."

In applying a legal resolution to a dispute or a transaction, you're often attempting to apply rationality to an emotional situation. If we push our chosen resolution when the timing is bad or beyond the boundaries of the parties' comfort zone, it can cause emotive behavior that is tough to reverse. First I try to ask questions like: What is the "must have" that the other side needs to take away? What can't we lose? It's very important to recognize what the limits are in a given solution set. Trespassing those limits may drive irrational behavior.

This is not as simple as it sounds. The person on the other side of the table will often have a broad position. But if you drill down it typically narrows into one or two things the person can't accept. They'll scorch the earth to avoid those two things. Sometimes the best way to ferret that out is to tell them what your position is: why you must have A or you can't have X. The more I do this, the more I recognize that the nature of our profession and craft is not just to advocate and espouse, but often to get the other party to articulate honestly what they really need.

In the head of legal role the issues that have found their way up the organization, and by that time there are usually entrenched positions and aligned constituencies, with real losses and gains on the table. You have to find a way to balance those as fast as possible.

Having Trust

You cannot operate effectively in your team without an environment of trust. It's first and foremost: a key Tenet. Trust usually takes a long time to build, and again, the General Counsel has no luxury of time. My lesson there is that you can't get trust from someone unless you actually give it to them.

I was lucky to be able to fill my organization here with people whom I deeply trust, and do that in such a way as to not create career bottlenecks or frustration in the organization. After networking and working with many people, I was ready to reach out and bring on board people that I trusted and knew could grow with the organization. People that will make it happen. It's essential to trust people's skills, have faith in their honesty and their judgment. It doesn't mean they won't make mistakes—we all do. But you have to share the trust, or the synergy of the team is severely limited.

My relationships with my outside counsel mirror what I seek internally: trust. If your main focus on outside counsel is on cost, you're almost defeated from every definition of partnering.

I want outside counsel that buy into a long-term relationship. Sometimes there won't be a lot for them to do, but I expect them to continue investing in understanding my business and my industry. Sometimes I have to let them know: "Here's what I have, money wise, and here's all I can give you to do." When we reach the same level of trust I have in my in-house team, my outside counsel become an extension of our legal department.

Setting the Agenda

Every General Counsel approaches this differently based on their personality, but you have to set the agenda because there is more work in any given day than you can humanly handle. You have to drill down to things that have the potential to be nuclear, and put your attention there first.

My priority has been to establish process. There's a cadence; a drumbeat of issues that arise in any organization, and you have to consistently respond and move forward to it. My deputy, who runs our legal operations, really understands how to structure and maintain a great process. It's a real luxury for me. In football terms, that allows me to be a 'roverback,' the player on the diamond defense. He goes forward where he sees scoring opportunities but also can drop back in defense to engage the opposition when counter attacked.

I'm good at ten-ball juggling—you have to be to do these jobs. The trick is to be flexible enough to let 3 bounce and handle the flaming ball. It's a relief and a necessity that top talent on my team is managing the disciplines of process.

As a leader, there is really no way to control your schedule. Despite your best attempts to set a schedule, something inevitably comes up to rearrange the whole day, sometimes the whole week. You have to ensure the maintenance of a structure, process and cadence for the legal team, at the same time that you accept that your own days will not be like that.

Priorities and Compromises

If you don't control your own days, you may ask, how do you find any work-life balance? Let's be honest about it: if you want to go for the gold, you have to redefine the question. I was at the Beijing Olympics as Lenovo was sponsoring. Not once in the dozens of interviews of Michael Phelps did anyone ask him how he kept a work-life balance. There was no balance at that moment. He was dedicated to a singular goal and he sacrificed other things.

Great feats are not accomplished by introducing a lot of life balance. You have to define the importance of what you're trying to accomplish within the context of your life at that time. Then you decide what you have to give up, at least for a while. Being the General Counsel of a major global company is not a 9 to 5 job. If you want to play at that level, you will have to set priorities.

Forget Being the Hero

A tenet to remember: If you want to lead, you have to enjoy other people's successes. You don't really get to enjoy your own very much. I truly believe I have the best legal department in the world, and it gets irritating to some of my functional brethren. In my enthusiasm they think I'm saying that my team is better than theirs.

When you're the General Counsel, if it all goes right it was supposed to. And if it goes wrong, it was the leadership's fault. Bringing the problem out from the jaws of death—if you're doing that at the top level, there's probably too much risk at every level of the organization.

The diving catch which we love so much, when all the odds are against us and the Texas Ranger shoots 'em all down and saves the day. Those victories will be won at a level or two beneath you. You have to enjoy that and not only point and cheerlead it, but truly get your juice from it.

The Importance of Culture

I had the good fortune of getting solid cross-cultural experience as head of legal for Europe, Middle East and Africa for Honeywell. It was wonderful training, because in Europe you're forced to deal with cultural issues every day. Cultures are so strong, proud and adamant in countries like France, Germany and Spain. They do not intend to disappear.

To do business and practice law you have to respect and try to understand cultural differences. You must operate within the cultural constructs, and if you don't, you can have the greatest legal solution in the world that simply will not play.

I learned a lesson early about the value of restraint. The law is a very blunt instrument in its finality, and it gets very tough in the end game. When we go to litigation, the step functions become draconian. The real power, like any other sort of organizational power, is in exercising your influence and getting something done without having to pull the trigger.

In a multicultural and multinational environment, exercising that power is far more complex. Your ability and influence is guided by understanding of available and appropriate behavior. You have to understand the typical business or legal construct for the circumstance.

In the 90's when I was in Europe, Americans made some big mistakes by coming in and saying, 'we're sort of running things here, let me show you how to do it." I was lucky to have local colleagues who encouraged me to work on position and persona: to seek to *understand* as opposed to *resolve*.

Now working with a company with major interests in China, the most difficult part is admitting ignorance of the history and the cultural drivers. Many of us have our point of reference in the West. As an American I lived in a multicultural group, the majority of which came from Western Europe, and it's easier for me to understand those cultural constructs. I'm always astounded at how much more the Chinese understand my culture

31

than I understand theirs. I've been reading the short, abridged History of China—it's 2 volumes, each with 36 chapters. The fundamentals of Chinese ways of thinking are difficult to grasp, and far more nuanced than what I have studied in the West. We have tons of writing about what Plato meant. To understand Chinese philosophies is a journey, and a hard one.

I've been in this position for 18 months, and I realize that the big challenge in China is to have the humility to recognize what I don't know. We cannot assume that we can apply in China the lessons we've learned elsewhere—certainly not in the same way. Language is a big barrier, and the time zones make it tough. There's a much steeper curve to building trust—both within the organization and with adversaries. It's a work in process and I find it exhilarating.

Fit for Global

One of the most surprising lessons I've learned in this job is that you need to be in shape physically to lead a global function. That is a part of the balance you can't forego. The travel and the hours will destroy your health if you're not careful about food, drink, sleep and exercise.

I sent my last email at 12.30 last night, so I knew today I wouldn't wake up at 5am and hit the gym. But I will work out sometime today, because if I don't keep myself in shape my schedule will run me down.

The days of jumping on a plane and trying all the wines are over. I get on the plane and sleep. Forget the great hotel with all its luxuries—you won't indulge in any of it. Book a hotel with a great pool or gym; it's an antidote to hours inside cabs and office rooms. Air travel is anything but seamless. Last week I got stuck in Narita in the middle of the night without a functioning Berry or phone. I wasn't even supposed to be in Japan, and I was wandering around trying to find out how to make a call. Many miles later I spent a few hours in the pool to de-stress and re-energize, which gave me new juice for the next day. To be able to roll with the flow you have to stay physically fit.

Learn New Lessons

In the end, the key Tenet is to be open to learning new lessons. You surely will, so you might as well welcome it. Keep questioning your assumptions, keep listening. There's a great Chinese saying: "May you live in interesting times." Well, here we are, living in completely unprecedented times. In this last year our global economy has changed beyond our wildest imaginations. Capitalism is being redefined. No doubt about it, we live in interesting times—lots of lessons left to learn, lots to be DONE. ●

6.
Musical Chairs: How Today's General Counsel Earns a Seat at the Top Executive Table

Tom Sabatino
Executive VP and General Counsel
Schering-Plough Corp., New Jersey

All in a Day's (Month's?) Work: The Role of the General Counsel

For most corporations, the General Counsel's job continues to evolve and expand. It is an increasingly important and demanding role, not suited for the timid or meek. Today, General Counsels face more challenges than ever.

Corporations rely upon the GC to take the necessary and difficult actions to ensure that their organizations act ethically and in compliance with the letter and spirit of the law, wherever they are around the world.

The GC operates in a highly complex regulatory environment, no matter the company's industry. Every facet of a company's operations is controlled in one way or another by law, regulation or custom. Globalization has made the management of companies far more complicated and requires the GC to understand the implications of operating internationally. Last but certainly not least, the GC must act as the ethical conscience of the company.

The role of many General Counsels has also expanded far beyond the traditional chief legal officer role. He or she is frequently involved in enterprise wide risk management, corporate value creation and preservation, and corporate social responsibility. The GC is one that many turn to in a time of crisis to help navigate the corporation through the myriad issues that may arise. Finally, the GC may have other non-legal groups reporting to him, such as government affairs.

In each of these roles, the GC not only must sit at the executive table but must frequently occupy multiple chairs. This game of "musical chairs" that the General Counsel engages in daily requires speed, flexibility and a cool head.

The Legal Specialist Chair

The General Counsel starts in the Legal Specialist Chair. It is his or her primary seat and the reason for being at the table.

As the head lawyer for the enterprise, the GC is expected to know a little about a lot of things. At a minimum, the role of General Counsel includes providing legal advice on a wide range of complex commercial issues, corporate governance, legal compliance, policy matters, risk management, intellectual property, employment matters and litigation management.

In a large organization, it is impossible to be an expert in all of the areas of law that may come before the GC, but he or she must be able to spot the key issues and provide business-centered advice on the important ones. Frequently, General Counsel and their legal team advise in many areas of the law that are not clear, concise, or well-developed. The successful GC will know where he or she needs to consult others or take time to think through the implications. The GC must be willing to say "I don't know," but also say, "I'll find out."

One of the most important roles of any leader is to build an "A" team, and the General Counsel is no exception. The GC must build a team of legal specialists with deep knowledge as well as business acumen. The GC must ensure that the internal and external resources of the legal team are aligned and organized to meet the immediate and long-term goals of the business. Talent management within a law function can be both challenging and time consuming. But it is perhaps the most rewarding for a GC when he or she builds a team of lawyers that are viewed as key business members of the Company.

The Trusted Advisor Chair

The GC's traditional role as chief legal counselor to the corporation has expanded beyond pure legal issues and legal risk assessment. The role now more commonly includes sole or shared responsibility for a broader number of corporate matters such as Federal and State policy and government affairs, crisis management and commercial or enterprise risk. This greater responsibility is an opportunity for the GC to influence corporate leadership and bring greater value to the business.

The GC can only take on these diverse issues by being intimately familiar with the business, products and markets of the Company. The GC must also build trust within the organization, spending time with the sales and marketing people, the research and development teams, the manufacturing operations and the customers. It is not by sitting in an office that he or she will get a feel for the business. The GC cannot spend all day reading documents or debating legal issues or strategy (although this surely is part of the role). It's crucial to get out in the field, travel around the world and see what is happening.

The GC as trusted advisor must also have good peripheral vision. He or she must be able to "see around corners" to spot the issues that may impact the business. While it is good to be able to react to a problem when it occurs, it is far better to anticipate problems, whether or not they are legal issues, and actively manage the business away from them.

As mentioned earlier, the GC needs a 'cool head' to be a trusted advisor, balancing multiple responsibilities in a professional and ethical manner. Every GC must act clearly on behalf of the corporate entity. The GC must be the most objective person at the table, setting the right tone and driving it from the top down. The General Counsel's diligence can help ensure the corporation's commitment to ethical conduct.

The Team Player Chair

A true partnership between the General Counsel, the CEO, and the senior business leaders is a key element to the GC's effectiveness. Developing good relationships and building credibility with key members of the executive management team is necessary for the GC. Being present and accounted for provides leadership and builds trust.

For a GC, the role of legal specialist and trusted advisor can sometimes create distance between the GC and the others on the management team. The need to give unbiased advice, especially when that advice may constrain the ability of a business partner to achieve all of his or her objectives, can impact the perception of the GC as a team player. That is why the successful GC must work doubly hard at getting to know his or her business partners. By understanding the context and the needs and desires of others managers, the GC can help craft solutions that will advance business objectives.

This requires a lot of listening and learning. Taking the time to understand the objectives of the business and the challenges it faces will frequently lead to a creative solution. It also can close the distance among the lawyer and the other members of the team. In fact, the GC can become the catalyst and focal point for the team. The GC must also be willing to participate in the decisions, not merely give the legally-permissible options. By crafting a business solution to a problem, the GC not only becomes an integral contributor on the team, but advances the goals of the company in a legal and compliant way.

The Leader Chair

Successful performance of the role of General Counsel today requires the constant balancing and synthesizing of potentially competing interests. A successful GC has honed the ability to carry out his responsibilities with keen judgment, an independent spirit, personal integrity and a passionate commitment to the corporation.

The GC that successfully occupies the chairs of legal specialist, trusted advisor and team player is inevitably called upon to sit in the chair as Leader, whether formally anointed or not. But that role requires attributes that have little to do with legal training, and more to do with the personal attributes above.

The GC as leader must exhibit passion. Although seemingly contradictory to the concept of an objective, balanced approach to problem solving, it is in fact the logical extension of it. Once a course of action is chosen, a leader gets his team to execute with passion, enthusiasm and integrity. The successful GC will be as strong an advocate as any member of the team in pushing forward with actions that advance the company's goals.

Personal and professional integrity is critical to any leader. It is even more so with the GC, as he or she is seen as the guardian of ethics and integrity for the corporation. It is crucial that the GC "walk the talk" when it comes to striving to do the right thing. The GC must have the strength of character to be the lone wolf if necessary, use keen judgment and maintain independence.

Musical Chairs

The General Counsel fulfilling his or her job today will have a seat at a number of chairs at the top executive table. Legal Specialist, Trusted Advisor, Team Player, Leader. Jumping from seat to seat is not always easy, and can be confusing for the GC and other players at the table. But this range of roles for the GC is a growing necessity. It is here where the General Counsel can play a pivotal part. It is at this table where business strategies and imperatives are debated and decided, and the General Counsel helps shape the success of the enterprise. ●

7.
Transcending Legal Expertise to Get to the Heart of Serving Global Clients

Helena Samaha
General Counsel- EMEA
AlixPartners, Paris

I moved to London in 1991 to do my LLM in Corporate and Commercial law, having gained my law degree in France. My main interest was international business law and so it seemed to make sense to get an "international" law education. Before moving to London, I had lived and studied in the Middle East, Europe and America, and was fluent in Arabic, French, English and conversational German. What was planned as a year in London eventually became 16 years.

I was initially sidetracked by the opportunity to train at Clifford Chance—and who would turn that down? It came about because, during my LLM, I started looking for work in Dubai, where my parents lived. The firm's policy was to train all recruits at the London headquarters, and so I extended my planned stay in London after my LLM. With Clifford Chance I trained across Finance, Corporate and Commercial and qualified into Finance, where I worked in the Securitisation group when

41

this practice was very prominent in the City of London. I took part in numerous cutting-edge, cross-border securitisation transactions for large mortgage providers, retailers, and credit card companies. It was not for the faint-hearted, and all-nighters were frequent.

Although I was fortunate to train and qualify in such a firm, I ultimately moved on because I was more interested in resolving a business' day-to-day legal issues than in complex, intangible financial structures.

So I went in-house, which raised lots of eyebrows back when the in-house lawyer was seen as the poor cousin of the private practitioner. I was warned that I would get bored and be isolated ... one can't possibly do interesting work in these circumstances!

As it turned out, I had seven fascinating years at Virgin Management, the HQ of the Virgin Group. As Group Legal Director, I worked on many innovative transactions spanning the four corners of the globe, in sectors including mobile virtual network operators and space tourism, or M&A in luxury hotels and game reserves. I explained Virgin's new services and argued our case for the unusual business models with regulators across North America, Europe and Africa. Many a challenge and never a dull moment.

I then did something less typical: I moved from a senior in-house position into partnership in a large global firm, DLA Piper. With the help of our purchasing function, at Virgin I had implemented one of the first formal law firm panels. My panel firms were very much a part of my legal team, and DLA Piper was one of them. Now in private practice, my role was to develop an internationally-focussed commercial practice out of London, covering Europe, Middle East and Africa (EMEA), with a focus on the Gulf.

If I had £10 for every time I was asked why I moved from in-house back to private practice, I would be retired now ... in the south of France, of course. Truth is, I was curious to work back in private practice, in particular as a partner, and I liked the global dimension of the firm and the opportunities it presented me.

At DLA Piper my attention was focussed on how to best serve global clients in an integrated way. The firm had a network of offices to do this. It also had a good approach to streamlining the work product and service offered everywhere, whilst embracing local business practices and providing local advice. This, coupled with my project management and international experience, seemed a good mix. I recorded a number of successes with like-minded colleagues across the network and together we converted some excellent US clients into global clients.

An ongoing challenge, in my opinion, is to create a viable business structure for the global law firm that recognizes the key value-add for corporate clients: international coordination of legal services. Most law firms have not done a great job of integrating   project management and the oversight of multi-jurisdictional work into their current business models, and it does not easily fit into the traditional law firm recognition and rewards mechanisms.

In 2007, my husband's offer of partnership with Ernst & Young in Paris presented me an opportunity to return to *La Cité Lumiere* where I had always hoped to live again. We left London in August 2007 to settle in Paris, and I joined AlixPartners as their General Counsel for EMEA.

AlixPartners is a leading global consultancy, specialising in performance improvement, turnaround and restructuring. We work in mostly high-impact, high-risk, time-critical situations. My role is to manage the risk around our engagements. Our clients are local or global and our people work wherever the clients are. While I knew little about this arena when I joined, my work experiences up to now have made me a quick study.

Recently an in-house counsel who had been my client at DLA Piper called to tell me that he had lost his job. He wanted to have a coffee and talk about next steps. "I have only ever worked in the same, narrow field of law," he said. "Specialised, not many market players. Any ideas where I go from here?" Without really thinking, I responded: "It doesn't matter so much the field of law or industry you've been in, but the skills you've developed in your work. You just need to figure out what they are and how to transfer them from one environment or role to the next."

Legal practitioners tend to structure their firms and perceive themselves according to geography, practice, or industry area. But when you work in a global business you acquire, and learn the vital importance of, commercial acumen, cultural understanding, remembering the bigger picture, strong communication skills (f you work for a successful CEO or entrepreneur, you usually have 30 seconds to get your message across!), the importance of relationships (many disputes are settled through the strength of relationships, not the courts) and above all... common sense!

In addition to the learnings from business, serving global clients requires flexibility and adaptability, which can be gained in combining different experiences. The skills are developed through working in private practice and then in business; or working in Europe, the Middle East and then the US, or Asia. Within law firms, it never ceased to amaze me how very little exposure non-partners got to the client development, pitching and billing scene. Yet these are critical skills to develop early, since a law firm must win clients like any other business. Conversely, one still rarely sees a senior lawyer or partner move geographically and adapt their practices accordingly.

Globalization makes it more important than ever to be able to relate to people where business practice and culture are different, never mind the language. Young lawyers should be encouraged to develop those skills which transcend legal expertise, industry sectors, and geographies. Some law departments are doing a good job of this already, partly because a range of skills are highly valued in the corporation, over and above satisfactory technical legal skills. From my current position I see how fluid people are in consultancies and how quickly businesses can evolve, and it seems that law firms are behind.

So, which is better, you might ask: inside or outside, and when will I settle with one or the other? Will I finally be a commercial lawyer, a turnaround lawyer or a finance lawyer? For me, those distinctions miss a key element of serving global clients today. The diverse experiences I have had, inside and outside, across sectors, practices and geographies, combine to make me more confident, versatile, and credible in the eyes of others. That's more valuable than the best narrow legal expertise imaginable. And from where I'm standing, it makes for a far more interesting career. ●

8.
Laws are Local: How Can Corporate Legal Services Become More Global?

Adam Smith
General Counsel
EADS Defence, Munich

These days, any self-respecting company needs to declare global ambitions. To be in tune with the Zeitgeist of the early 21st Century, one must ramp up one's presence in China, India, the Middle East, and North Africa... So, in corporate legal departments around Europe, we lawyers nod sagely and promise that we will accompany our clients on these exotic projects. Of course, most of the lawyers are Europeans like me, with little or no exposure to the legal systems of those places. So (like all good professionals) we make it up as we go along and hide our copy of "Libyan Law for Dummies" under a pile of learned papers.

We feel comfortable doing so, because actually laws are not just local. In fact many of the laws that we deal with are already broader in scope than the jurisdiction of the particular project (e.g. EU-laws, contracts based on UN standards, or the jurisdiction-neutral documents of entities such as ISDA or the ICC). Or they are the laws of another country anyway, for example US arms-control regulations.

Moreover, the continental-style agreement where the parties rely on some arcane Napoleonic code to fill in all the drafting they couldn't be bothered to do runs counter to my Anglo-Saxon training. I like to see a nice long agreement that contains all its own legislation, like one of those fine-print dictionaries that comes with its own magnifying glass. With everything you need to know already written in the agreement, who needs local law?

So, much of the content of an in-house lawyer's job is outside our home jurisdiction, but we don't mind. After all, we don't need to be experts; we can outsource that. We're supposed to be legal project managers.

In fact this divergence between technical expertise and management mindset creates a tension that big legal departments are starting to feel. International companies expect their senior staff to be mobile: you only get the key to the executive washroom if you have experience of plumbing systems in several countries. When I objected to one HR director that lawyers are one of the least re-locatable resources in a company and that we should be excluded from such rules, he pointed out that my own example disproved my argument. I have already been a lawyer in three jurisdictions and I'm only just out of short trousers.

Lawyers can move but only if, like me, they have a weak grasp of detail. I can be a technically impoverished lawyer anywhere in the world, not just in England. We should probably stop worrying about how to move lawyers who are anyway no longer doing much law and instead focus on how to retain and motivate those skilled specialists who really would be no use outside their home jurisdiction. For this, we need to lay out some kind of "expert" career path that diverges from the management route, so that these valuable but non-transferable people don't get stranded. Technical expertise is often undervalued in the corporate environment, where having a Type-A personality is more important than being able to remember the exceptions to the *nemo dat quod non habet* rule, but sometimes you want advice from someone with a big throbbing brain, not a big throbbing Mercedes.

Outsourcing the local component by hiring lawyers on the ground is of course usually safer than the *Dummies* guide when it comes to advising management whether that Libyan contract is actually valid or not. Thankfully, we have two models to choose from: the big Anglo-

Saxon law firm that recently mopped up half the local hotshots and is manfully forcing them to use PowerPoint, or the other half of the hotshots who still think they can make a living from membership in some nebulous network that nobody can pronounce. Both are valuable: it's a comfort to know there's someone in the City you can kick if things start going wrong in Ulan Bator. But sometimes you prefer the tranquillity of working with the local guru in Tashkent who isn't then going to try to sell you her firm's capabilities in Quito. (Don't these firms realise I can look Quito up in a book and find out for myself who's any good?)

In the days before telephones and email, a company would send its agent to an exotic location fully empowered to broker a deal without contacting HQ. Now, technology means we can keep the power at home (we say we are "thinking globally") and move our local pawns around by BlackBerry. But as IT increasingly makes expertise a commodity, will we need local lawyers at all when we can find a commentary to the civil code of Tajikistan on Wikipedia? The answer is, of course, yes. We will still need people to sit in data rooms, people to fill in planning permission applications, and someone to give us their discounted rate in the Hilton. After all, laws may be increasingly global but you don't want to try to enforce an Anton Piller order by videoconference. ●

9.
Reflections on Moving Inside to Outside: My Favorite Outside Lawyers When In-House, My Favorite Clients Today

Bruno Cova
Partner
Paul Hastings Janofsky and Walker LLP, Milan

I returned to private practice in 2005 after a 13-year absence, during which time I was General Counsel of the Exploration & Production Division of Eni, Chief Compliance Officer of the European Bank of Reconstruction and Development (EBRD) and Group General Counsel of Fiat, and after acting as the chief legal adviser during the Parmalat crisis (a special project from 2003-2005 that was not truly in-house nor private practice).

In most cases, particularly in complex matters, a corporation needs cooperation between the in-house legal function and outside counsel. I came to Paul Hastings fully convinced that it is good to have seen and worked from both sides of the equation. As inside or outside counsel you develop skills that make it possible to do your job better, whatever your job is. If you have been part of both segments of the "production line," you naturally have more information to contribute to the whole process.

A Piece in the Jigsaw Puzzle

As a private practitioner, I see my role as providing input and completion to the product that the General Counsel is delivering within the company.

My in-house experience has made it simple to draw the mental map necessary to identify the client's objective for each assignment. It is important to understand exactly what the in-house legal function is able to do *itself* without outside support, and where as outside counsel we can add value. My work as outside counsel is a piece in a jigsaw puzzle, the shape of which is created by the in-house counsel.

This view may not be obvious to lawyers who have only worked in private practice. Having worked my way up to the General Counsel role in large and diversified companies, I am accustomed to spotting multi-disciplinary issues and managing multi-disciplinary themes. The challenge then is to understand what is needed to address and advise on those issues. There is often know-how within the company that I do not need to duplicate, so that I can then effectively complete the in-house team's available skills and resources with what else is needed.

For example, if there is a tax angle, I raise it with the General Counsel, and ask him if his tax people have it covered or if we should cover it outside. If they want us to cover it, I bring in a member of our team.

Global Vantage Point: Legal and Business

Another plus to having been on both sides is the truly global vantage point, for both legal and business issues. If you are General Counsel in a global group, everything has an international element. It becomes a frame of mind, a natural consideration that you bring to private practice. Outside counsel in various jurisdictions often do not take foreign law issues into account, and that can really discount their advice. They may be part of a global law firm, or of an alliance of law firms, but few truly and consistently work in a cross-border context. It is entirely different from merely providing domestic law advice in a foreign language, or drafting a contract in English.

In-house counsel gain more managerial experience than private practitioners typically do. Within the company we repeatedly allocate tasks, define a game plan, spot side issues and future challenges, advise management on reporting of various information to different constituencies, and define the deliverable. This background is useful to me now. For example, there are instances when the client needs a lengthy legal opinion because of the circumstances and the nature of advice requested. Sometimes another type of output suits: a flowchart, a conference call, slides for the directors of the company, or a check-list.

Having been in-house allows me to be more effective in understanding what the company's real requirements might be, and in proactively suggesting options to the client. Since I am naturally more confident in my understanding of what the client really needs, I can go back and say "Before we start working on this, I just wanted to check…" and then make a suggestion that may help reduce or resolve the problem.

Client Preferences

The clients that I generally appreciate working with are those General Counsel that are powerful within their corporation and are managing a strong legal function. They have performed well and are respected by their management, and they have quick access to the kind of information I may need. They understand why the corporation is using me, and this makes them better able to sell what we are doing together within the company.

I appreciate clients that are straightforward. It must be an honest relationship: if I am doing something they do not like I want to know as soon as possible so that I can take corrective action and improve. When I do something right, it is nice and useful if they let me know I am on the right course.

I like in-house lawyers that stick to their side of the deal. It is simply unfair when a client expects you and your team to jump to a teleconference on a Sunday, and then pays your bills several months later and after many reminders. It is disrespectful.

I welcome clients who accept that the law is not always an exact science and are ready to take risks. Clients are becoming more sophisticated, and some—particularly hedge funds and other financial markets players—will tell me up front that they initially do not want me to do any lengthy legal research. First they want to have a teleconference to get my reading of the overall situation. In those situations the advice is quick, and the value to the client can sometimes be more the experience than the technical legal analysis.

It is a good thing when clients understand that they *can* get this from outside counsel. However, they must also accept the terms under which outside counsel can do so. In those circumstances, we cannot present it as a definitive legal response. It is a very cost effective way to get what, 80 percent of the time, is right and is *enough*. As experienced lawyers, often our first instinct is the correct one, and the memo that takes lots of time ends up simply confirming it.

Among the qualities I like best in a client are decisiveness and clarity. Those who manage the process and can really identify what they need from you get great value from their outside counsel. I recently experienced this in supporting an M&A transaction for a major international company, working with a very good in-house lawyer that heads M&A. After one teleconference and one meeting, she understood that the presence on the matter of someone with my seniority was not necessary, and that most aspects of a large due diligence effort could be handled in-house. She was happy to continue with a member of my team on those areas where she wanted the firm's advice and services, and otherwise she led the project overall.

By doing this, and doing the bulk of the due diligence internally, this in-house counsel reduced the cost to her company dramatically, and she made sure that key know-how stayed in the company. Meanwhile she accepted that my firm would only take responsibility for what we had actually been asked to do, and not for all the aspects of the transaction.

It is back to the jigsaw concept: we were able to provide the missing pieces. Some outside counsel would think this was an unfortunate outcome where billable hours were lost. I think it is the opposite. It was a profitable project for us, and yet the client made significant savings. I am better off leveraging the work of our associates, and adding more value to the firm by focusing on bespoke work that demands my experience.

Outside Counsel Preferences

On the flip side, now in private practice it helps to remember when I was General Counsel the outside lawyers I preferred, and why.

I liked the lawyers that showed a genuine interest in working for my company. You can understand quickly the level of homework outside counsel have done on the corporation and its legal function. I was impressed when the outside counsel showed that he or she had gained a sense of what had been done in the past and what the company's objectives were.

Then as now, I liked lawyers who were straight, honest and trustworthy. It comes through in big and small ways. For example, it was really detrimental to find out that outside counsel was not making me aware of a conflict of interest, or was not entirely truthful about his ability to deliver by a certain date or on the range of skills available in his team. These behaviors are not difficult to discover and are invariably a big problem, as they damage the core of the relationship: trust.

What I did not like as a General Counsel was working with outside lawyers that did not understand that they were part of MY machine. Instead they thought my company was part of THEIR machine. Occasionally I saw outside counsel who acted as though scoring points on opposing counsel was more important than reaching my objectives as client. I always found that pretty intolerable.

I wanted outside counsel to understand that legal instructions must only come from the legal function, not management. I continue to abide by that rule in private practice, always confirming with the General Counsel any instruction that may have come from another function. I regard this as a fundamental tenet of the unwritten rules of our profession, and the only way to be able to truly help the corporation and have access to all the information I need. Investigating the Parmalat fraud has also taught me how by-passing the legal function can be indicative of wrongdoing.

The biggest surprise in moving inside to outside is the opposite of what I suspected: it is not a big change at all. There are many similarities in what I used to do as a General Counsel and what I do now as a private practitioner. We just see things from different perspectives. Every bit of my in-house experience contributes to the success of my current practice, and helps me and my clients. I am happy with that equation. ●

10.
Understanding the Importance of Culture in Managing a Global Law Firm Effectively

Alan Jenkins
Chairman
Eversheds, LLP, London

A Finn is having a few days holiday in England with a British friend. They go to a typical pub for a few drinks. The Englishman orders "2 pints of bitter please." It is soon the Finn's turn to buy a round of drinks. He goes to the bar and puts the glasses down on the counter. "Beer," he says. The barman looks at him with a frown. "Will that be a half, a pint or a bucket?" says he, sarcastically.

All people are different. The Finn in that anecdote was behaving as he would at home, where such abrupt requests are the norm. The British, on the other hand, and the English in particular, would be offended by what they see as rudeness, having no experience of the different way in which Finns use language.

We know that all people are different, even within our own cultures, but how deeply do we accept this and act upon it? In trying to build an international law firm which is truly cohesive and provides integrated services to clients so that they have the same experience of the firm's services wherever they are, we must accept these inevitable differences and reconcile them.

Differences Provide an Advantage

This is a not an independent exercise. It is an integral part of building a successful firm in which the rich diversity of talent amongst the lawyers and staff finds its natural outlets regardless of ethnic origin, religion, age, gender, sexual orientation, and disability. Just as our firm is a kaleidoscope of differences, so are our clients. We have a vision to be a great place to work and the most client-centred international law firm. In order to be a great place to work, we must respect people for what they can do, regardless of how that differs from the traditional stereotype of the white male lawyer. Moreover, we can deploy that difference to the advantage of the client, the individual and the firm, and we seek actively to do so.

In the last few years we have built a large and successful business in the Middle East. This has been done in response to increasing demands for assistance from clients outside the region and also to take advantage of the opportunities for work back in Europe or in Asia for clients within the region. The mix of clients is therefore both of Arab and non-Arab origin.

A human characteristic is that people relate best to those who are like them, who understand them, listen to them, and speak to them in their own language. It is not always possible to find all these attributes in one person, but it is usually possible to find them in combination in a number of people. Thus, we have always sought in all our offices to have a mix of locally-qualified as well as international lawyers. Amongst the latter, we try to have colleagues who are of the local nationality, speak the language, share the local religion and so forth.

For example, in the Gulf, the head of our Islamic finance and banking practice is an English qualified lawyer, of Pakistani origin who speaks a little Arabic and is a practicing Muslim. He has an understanding of Sharia principles which is of a different order to that of a non-Muslim, who is likely to have merely an intellectual appreciation of them. In some ways more important even than this, though, is that he regularly attends Friday prayers at a mosque. The mosque is not just a religious place but also a social one, just as a synagogue may be for Jews or a church for Christians. By mixing with other Muslim businessmen at or after Friday prayers, bonds are established and relationships nurtured. These spill over into the business arena to the benefit of the work for clients and for the firm in developing new business.

On the other hand, expatriates may well feel happier, even subconsciously, in dealing with people like them. The mix allows us to try to meet all requirements, but in reality there also has to be a crossover. If expatriates are to be happy and productive working in places like the Gulf, China or Estonia, they have to have an appreciation of and empathy with the cultural norms of the place, even if the language is beyond them. To this end, each of our lawyers and other staff going to work in a country foreign to their own is given cultural awareness training, beyond what is available online or in books. Indeed, we hope that those going to foreign places will want to learn about such differences and our selection process includes a consideration of their cultural empathy.

At "Home" or "Abroad"

It is not all, however, about those working in "foreign" places. There is just as much a need to learn to work together when the client or colleague is of a different culture, even without leaving a domestic office. For some years there has been a wonderful, often humorous advertising campaign for HSBC which I often see in airports. It promotes the bank's global reach and capability combined with local knowledge through subjective interpretations of repeated, juxtaposed images. For example, an image of an American with his feet up on a desk and showing the soles of his shoes can be interpreted as bad manners and a sign of disrespect, or it can interpreted as a sign that he is relaxed and open. The images and differing interpretations in that campaign summarize very well what this article is about.

We can observe that our American friends often have an apparently relaxed and informal approach to management structures and hierarchy. Much of the rest of the world does not. The Germans like order and structure. In Japan, respect to the person with seniority commands respect to hierarchy and one does not disagree or debate in public. This is a lesson which has often to be learned by bitter experience.

At our firm some years ago, advice from our Italian office was urgently and unexpectedly required for a client in connection with a transaction taking place in the UK. The UK partner asked a trainee to send an email to the Milan managing partner seeking the help needed. The email was terse and peremptory and demanded the advice within a short deadline. It was badly received in Italy and caused disruption. Simple courtesy may have diminished its impact, but also an appreciation that in many parts of the world a telephone call followed by an email would be more effective than a short, cold email from a junior lawyer to a senior partner.

This little anecdote also touches on an important notion in legal services delivery: time. Perceptions of time are culturally biased. In Anglo-Saxon cultures, time is precious and requires things to be done expeditiously so that it is not wasted. In other cultures, such as China, time is part of the context and a factor amongst others to be taken into account. Some years ago, we were applying for a licence in China. The time stipulated by the law for the authorities to have made a decision had expired. When questioned by one of our English colleagues for the umpteenth time why there was this delay and what could be done about, our Chinese colleague replied with some exasperation that we could indeed sue the authorities but that would not be wise. He added that we simply had to understand that to the Chinese, with a civilisation going back 7,000 years or more, time was a relative concept. Fifty years was a longish time; 6 months is a short time. Patience was required. What were a few months in a relationship that could last for years?

Pointers for Managing a Global Firm

So how do we manage a global law firm so that our services are integrated and our people work together effectively? Here are a few pointers:

- recruit for attitude

- treat cultural awareness holistically as an integral part of the way to do things; it runs alongside diversity programmes, marketing and business development, communications, and the day-to-day detail of the way we work together;

- do not presume that because English is the language of

58

international business, everyone who speaks it understands it fully, still less all the idioms and nuances we use. This is especially true for British English speakers, who are notorious for using euphemisms to lessen the impact of what they wish to say, out of a profound sense of politeness. I have witnessed a lawyer say "that is an interesting proposal" when he was politely trying to dismiss it, whilst his foreign counterpart thought he meant it was an idea which had merit and should be explored further.

• train people to be alive to these issues. They cannot be familiar with all the differences between each of them and others from different backgrounds, but they can assume that there will be differences and incorporate that into their behaviour. This training is an integral part of induction and, for several years now, those going through our development centres on the partnership track have had sessions on these issues.

• make it easy for lawyers and staff to learn about how a person from a different race, religion or country might behave or look upon a transaction; there are many resources available today, whether they be books, DVDs or online

• bear in mind that this is a journey; the larger the firm and the more widespread the locations, the more difficult but also the more crucial the journey is.

In addition to these measures, management should set the example, by our own diversity and by being attentive to cultural differences, being ready and willing to learn and adapt. Without this integration, global service delivery is an empty promise. ●

11.
The Signature Legal Challenge of the 21st Century

Peter J. Kalis
Chairman and Global Managing Partner
K&L Gates LLP, New York

There is much written these days about the challenges facing the legal profession. Views differ, but in essence the perceived challenges range from strategic positioning to optimal pricing with many stops in between. Although it is always helpful to describe the tensions that at once burden and invigorate our professional lives as lawyers, it may be useful to elevate the perspective to a level of abstraction not typically focused on by in-house or law firm lawyers.

At the risk of indulging heresy, it seems to me that the signature legal challenge of the 21st Century is not unique to our profession. It's not even unique to our clients. Rather, it's an all-embracing challenge that can torment and energize clients and law firms but far transcends their existence. For us, it is a 'legal' challenge. In fact, it is as unique to law as breathing.

The signature challenge to which I refer is the movement of people, products, services and capital across borders. With breathtaking velocity, our commercial world is washing away the significance of nation-states. National boundaries are increasingly commercial curiosities—vestiges of time past—with one critical exception: Each national boundary triggers the applicability of different legal regimes, and each legal regime is a cluster of arcane legal rules with glosses of interpretation not necessarily perceptible from the outside. From a legal standpoint, the world is teeming with scores of traps for the unwary.

More generally, this signature challenge forces a re-examination of national sovereignty, modalities of international cooperation, demographic and workforce projections, climate change and fusion cuisine, among other transcendent issues. But for the legal profession, the issues are tightly focused, even narrow in nature, yet profoundly important to us and all whom we serve.

As a profession, are we aligned to facilitate the *lawful* and *efficient* movement of people, products, services and capital across borders? We live in an age in which, for example, even modest-sized enterprises compete in global markets. As a profession, have we aligned our businesses to address their legal requirements?

For great global corporations, is your legal function poised to address both local requirements in far-flung jurisdictions as well as rules relating to cross-border movements? Have you developed relationships with providers that can serve you seamlessly across borders?

As law firms and law departments try to figure out how to address different legal regimes separated only by imaginary lines, they should gain confidence by drawing upon a key precedent. Although greatly influenced by an overlay of Federal constitutional and statutory law, the 50 US States and the District of Columbia run concurrent and largely autonomous legal systems, and the profession long ago adjusted to this phenomenon.

Not true, you say? Consider the recent (legal) activities of the Office of the Attorney General of New York. At times, that state function has made the SEC seem second fiddle. Or reflect upon the perils of going to trial in a pharmaceutical liability case in various state courts in the US. FDA approval for your drug may seem quite weak protection at this point, at least until the US Supreme Court rules on the subject.

Think of state-based systems of taxation, employment regulation, environmental control, and countless other distinct rules, including rules of pleading, evidence, and case management. The fundamentally cross-border character of practicing law in the US is so ingrained that we take it for granted. Clearly, however, it has shaped the minds and approaches of generations of lawyers, law firms and law departments.

What did we do? We aligned our law firms and our law departments to meet these challenges. Law firms grew into national organizations that operated efficiently across political boundaries, and law departments relied on these aligned firms and complemented them with local expertise where needed. This market-based change occurred with not a lot of gnashing of teeth. The movement was evolutionary and largely effective and efficient.

The difference now is the pace of globalization and the radical differences in legal systems and surrounding cultures. The constitutional overlay in the US turns out to be significant, as do the legal priorities in Sovereign States. On the latter point, as one of many examples, just consider the employment law regime in France. It is a political and cultural priority for that nation, and it represents a significant departure from the approaches of many other Sovereign States. The expertise to deal with such challenges must be "on the ground."

For law firms, the challenge translates this way: Align your business with the businesses of clients and potential clients in an era of intense globalization and consolidation, or risk the peril of obsolescence. For corporate law departments, encourage your law firm partners to serve you in the way you do business in the 21st Century—not the way that law firms did business in the 20th Century. ●

12.
The Role of Law Firm Values in Successful Global Expansion

Despina Kartson
Chief Marketing Officer
Latham & Watkins LLP, New York

I've spent the last five of my 20 year legal services career at Latham & Watkins, and during that time I have seen the firm expand globally, increase in attorney numbers, increase revenue and continue to invest in pro bono, diversity, client and career development opportunities for women and corporate social responsibility. As Latham & Watkins celebrates its 75th birthday, I've been reflecting on the values of the firm, past and present, that carry us forward. Values might be overlooked in the constant juggle of priorities of any business today, yet, from the business development perspective, these values are central to everything we do, and thus the subject of this essay.

Our firm has a consistent culture that was put in place and has been spreading its roots since Latham & Watkins was founded 75 years ago. One of the initial and fundamental tenets is that we are truly a meritocracy. This means that lawyers and staff are given fair and equal opportunities to contribute. Their input is not only asked for but welcomed. For example, our associates are involved in the recommendations and decision-making process for hiring and promoting other associates. Many recognize that this level of input is rare.

In my five years at the firm, our chairman, Bob Dell, has always emphasized the firm's values and culture in presentations to the partners and associates. In fact, the importance of our culture is informally and formally articulated and repeated by all of our senior management.

There are three key elements:

People
Performance
Governance

With **people** we focus on teamwork, a collegial professional environment, integrity and professional responsibility. For employees, morale is high, our people take pride in their work and they go the extra mile. If you asked a number of Latham employees, I think they would agree that we have a solid firm culture and the highest quality people. This quality and responsiveness naturally extends to the service we provide our clients.

When it comes to **performance** we believe there should be no compromise on quality, both in terms of technical legal support, project staffing (a lot of partner involvement) and service delivery. Partners and all firm employees are regularly reviewed and given feedback on their performance. Firm leadership also spends a lot of time talking to clients about how we're performing.

Our **governance** is based on a "one firm" principle. We do not have a headquarters and we do not view offices as individual profit centers. The firm is very transparent with information, with a lot of detail shared at the partner and associate levels.

Because of our meritocracy in which everyone is invited to contribute, decision making does not take place in a vacuum. We spend time discussing and tweaking major decisions. Sometimes we pilot a major move on a smaller scale, and then evolve it based on our experience.

This process might appear to bog down decisions, but taking the time to do this up front often makes what follows flow far more smoothly. It keeps us connected, which is key to the one-firm premise, with so much work that crosses borders. For example, the real estate lawyers from our European offices are working with lawyers in our Moscow office, or lawyers in New York and London are working on matters with lawyers from our three offices in the Middle East.

It's important that our values don't get lost as we expand, or we would lose our key differentiators among peer firms. People look at us as a firm rather than a collection of individual offices – which is precisely how we operate. In fact, our values and culture and their connection to the Latham brand has solidified as we've grown. A key element of this solidity is our tradition of moving people from existing offices to our new offices. They transport the cultural elements, translate the concepts to the local environment, and the roots are thus reinforced.

People Keep Values Alive

Keeping our values alive as we grow must be part and parcel of our business development efforts. It has a lot to do with the type of people that we bring into the firm; whether they're in a completely new market to us or a very well developed market. We prioritize getting the right fit, because we want to continue to grow the firm with people of like mind.

For example, if a lateral partner is being considered, he or she will do a "world tour" and meet with partners all around the firm. This happens with our key management positions as well. These candidates, in addition to their first rate legal skills, must also reflect our core values.

Much of this might sound vague, but it is backed by specific approaches and processes. Everyone who joins Latham & Watkins participates in a detailed training and orientation program. In the Business Development department, we share our standardized messages with attorneys, and then we continually communicate the firm's messages in our day-to-day interaction.

Our approach is to have high quality, senior marketing professionals managing the business development and marketing efforts in our markets. Our structure and our processes provide plenty of support to coordinate working at two levels: global and local.

We also work very hard to support our managers in Asia and the Middle East who are the sole marketers in their offices. Though they are physically far away, we have strong communication and methods in place so that they never feel too remote or out of the loop. They reach out to get help from local and global peers as necessary. No matter how busy we all are, someone always pitches in.

Global Consistency

In marketing and many other areas, the impact of our consensus approach is that we constantly must balance global consistency with local circumstances. As head of marketing, I recognize and accept certain pushback. Some things are simply not appropriate in a certain market. Sometimes an argument will be presented and I'll acquiesce, in other areas, almost never. For example, there's no give on quality or behavior of our team.

As the firm expands internationally, we try to keep continuity through shared values and do this without dampening our entrepreneurial spirit. Some of this we accomplish through classic marketing and branding efforts. A few examples:

> • The look and feel of Latham offices are consistent around the world. The office space has a similar design and décor, receptionists greet guests in the same way, the signage and placement is consistent.

> • Our technology infrastructure is also consistent worldwide. It continues to impress me when I go from office to office that my laptop plugs in and connects me to the network with the same ease.

> • We have brand rules and style guides for our visual materials and we have marketing staff responsible to ensure these rules are followed. Every month I receive a set of the final versions of every piece published in every office, so I keep an eye on it all. The consistency within the department is evident when, for example, a practice group description is revised, and the style and tone taken is in line with other practice descriptions.

These core values are fundamental and timeless, and they won't change over time, space, or size of firm. Everything about our brand and our marketing execution takes those values to heart. Our clients are global, and the need for us to be able to support them is ever-present and growing. We will adapt and change as the rest of the global economy changes and continue to be a firm with a global footprint, where we can provide all of the services that we provide anywhere in the world. ●

13.
International Pro Bono:
Broadening our Geographical Reach

Chris Marshall
Pro Bono & Community Manager, Reed Smith
and Chair, Board of Trustees
Advocates for International Development, London

When it comes to contributing skills to help others, lawyers are in an eminent position. Lawyers' contributions often remain unrecognized, especially outside of the profession. However, within it, there is a strong and growing sense that lawyers are under a particular obligation: an imperative to share the knowledge and the talents that we have for free for the good of the wider community.

Who then is our wider community? Traditionally the response has been our immediate neighbour. Many law firms, large and small, started as general practices, part of a local community, working in a world where marketing could only be by word of mouth. In such circumstances, lawyers knew those locally who were in need. Assisting the deserving was part and parcel of being a member of that local community. It was also, in terms of keeping one's firm at the heart of the community, the financially prudent thing to do. A reputation as someone who would offer a helping hand, who would assist when times were hard encouraged new and underpinned longer term relationships; it provided a sustaining link with fee-paying clients.

The situation for both lawyers and for pro bono today is, in many ways, strikingly different. Many firms have moved beyond their local community base. Most lawyers are deeply specialized in their practice. Advertising, in many jurisdictions, is now a fact of life and clients, in many cases, are concerned with clients and communities across the globe. The same is true for those working in-house. In the midst of this, pro bono has advanced—it has moved beyond the things that a lawyer does within his or her own spare time in response to their conscience. Many firms operate pro bono and community programmes run by dedicated staff across multiple offices, involving the foregoing of millions in fee-earning time. A changing landscape has emerged.

My first pro bono opportunity came as I was about to enter law school. Instead of living in the usual student accommodation, I opted to move into a residential community centre in central Nottingham, England. The experience was a turning point. Seeing first hand the benefits that a lawyer's skills can bring—helping to draft employment contracts for local charities, advising community groups on governance structures, etc —gave a fresh perspective to my studies.

Many of the issues that lawyers see in their local communities, and which were areas of acute need during my year in Nottingham, are equally, if not more, significant in the wider world. Law is fundamental to many things in life—it creates the system that registers our birth; it provides the right to access healthcare and education and sets the standards we can expect; it protects us within the workplace and enables us to bring in capital to start our own business; to own property; and to pass on these assets when we die. In the absence of a functioning legal system, it is the essentials of life, rather than luxuries that suffer.

The Link Between Law, Poverty & Exclusion

In mid 2008 the Commission on the Legal Empowerment of the Poor produced its report. The Commission, which was co-chaired by Madeleine Albright and Hernando de Soto, was backed by the personal commitment of over 20 world leaders and was established to be a catalyst for change on the tackling of poverty issues. The Commission was the first global organization to focus on the significance of the link between law, poverty and exclusion. The culmination of a long process of meetings and questions with ordinary people in developing countries, the report's conclusions are striking:

> "...at least 4 billion people are excluded from the rule of law. It is the minority of the world's people who can take advantage of legal norms and regulations. The majority of humanity is on the outside looking in."[1]

Whilst a number of those that the Commission identifies will be within our local communities, most are not. To address their needs it is important that lawyers look beyond local and national boundaries. This is a process that has already begun and one which must be carried out in co-ordination with ongoing, locally focused pro bono projects. With many lawyers not yet involved in pro bono, extending boundaries should not mean a choice between international or domestic work. Instead, it offers the promise of new opportunities in new areas. These extend to lawyers of all ages and levels of expertise, irrespective of jurisdiction and practice area and whether they are in private practice or in-house. If you are a funds lawyer, there is scope to advice on the creation of new global donors; if a tax lawyer, to assist on remittances to Africa; and if an international investment expert, to work with governments on ensuring that investment is pro development.

Lawyers Provide Invaluable Insights

Last year in Santiago, Chile, a group of international non-governmental organizations (NGOs) and the UN Economic Commission on Latin America with assistance from Advocates for International Development (A4ID), brought together the international investment teams from every Latin American country except Venezuela. Our aim in doing so was to share knowledge on investment issues across the region, inform investment negotiators of the implications and significance of terms and support government lawyers in dealing with investment disputes. Sessions were led by academics, NGO lawyers, policy experts and very significantly by private practice lawyers assisting pro bono. Each component of the course was important, but private practice lawyers added the very valuable experience of working with both "sides." By explaining what they would do if advising an investor, as well as describing how they would work with a client government, the lawyers not only provided an invaluable insight into the complexities of international investment, they also contributed in line with their core skills.

From jurisdiction to jurisdiction rules govern who may and who may not be assisted pro bono. Often the focus is around the client's means, the nature of the project and the nature or mission of the client. It is rare in international pro bono for clients to be individuals. In acting for States or international not-for-profits or intergovernmental organizations, difficult decisions have to be taken on pro bono eligibility. Should a government, which will instruct lawyers on a fee-paying basis and which "must" have funds, ever be advised pro bono? What is the case for supporting an international commission, such as the Commission on Legal Empowerment, or a global development organization?

These are undoubtedly difficult questions. On a par is the issue of how to ensure that the small not-for-profit organization that approaches you from a post conflict zone is who it says it is. These challenges are peculiarly international pro bono focused. They are difficult questions, but they can and must be answered as we seek to extend the global reach of pro bono.

The Pro Bono Broker

In domestic pro bono many law firms typically source their own opportunities. As a result of complex needs in wide ranging jurisdictions and cultures, this is less the case in international pro bono. Given the complexity of issues and cross-cultural challenges, many firms have found that a pro bono "broker" can be of great assistance. By conducting thorough due diligence, reviewing and analysing the resources and mission of the client and researching the scope of the actual request, a broker makes sure that these questions are answered. Among the international pro bono organizations are: Advocates for International Development, International Senior Lawyers Project, PILI (Public Interest Law Institute) and the Cyrus

Vance Centre. The broker also assists with the crucial work of ensuring that the lawyers' assisting are both prepared to address the nuances of the situation, and that their contribution has the impact that the hard work involved deserves. The broker is there to enable the lawyers to focus on doing what they do best – high quality pro bono work.

Sometimes a visit to a potential partner is needed to effectively scope a pro bono project, and this is often the function of the pro bono broker. Through a global partner, A4ID was approached by Mkombozi and the Arusha Caucas on Child Rights, both based in Tanzania. With these organizations' focusing on how to protect the rights of street children, there was an obvious case for pro bono involvement. What was not clear was how international lawyers could contribute. As Chairman of A4ID, I travelled to Arusha to meet Mkombozi's Children's Programs' Coordinator, Shermin Moledina, to find out more. After meeting with Shermin, the other members of the Caucas and seeing Mkombozi's work in action, two things were clear. In addition to confirming a compelling need for lawyers to assist pro bono; we also identified specific tasks that an international team could fulfill, working alongside local lawyers. The role of the broker then is to assist in building rapport, clarify the specific pro bono project parameters and importantly to make sure any new project takes account of previous pro bono, including that done by others.

In-house Counsel's Role in Pro Bono

The pro bono landscape extends beyond the private practice lawyer/pro bono client relationship. Corporations and their in-house teams have always had a role to play. The local business that valued the support its lawyers gave to those in need has now been replaced by the global business that wants its lawyers' pro bono priorities to resonate with its own corporate responsibility programmes.

Initiatives such as Make Poverty History and the United Nations Millennium Development Goals (MDGs), together with increased political and social activism, have led global corporations to become more focused on global need. Most recently with the United Nations Development Programme (UNDP) and the UK Government's Business Call to Action, leading multinationals declared their support and active involvement in the fight against global poverty. The Business Call to Action is not about philanthropy. It challenges companies to use their core business —whether it is manufacturing, finance, telecommunications—in a way that contributes both to the MDGs and to their commercial success... By building a safer and more prosperous world, businesses are securing future commercial success."[1]

Most international pro bono opportunities are available to all lawyers. Projects, such as the review of proposed legislation in Afghanistan on women's rights, training microfinance institutions in the Middle East and North Africa on standard terms of commercial loan agreements and advice on land rights issues for the Batwa in Burundi, require skills found equally within in-house teams and law firms. Although there can be political sensitivities in corporations taking on some matters, the need is so great and the volume of opportunities so significant that there is work available for all. With matters ranging from those which are desk based and only require a few hours of time through to longer term commitments, there is something to suit every workload. Through international pro bono there are also good opportunities to align an in-house legal team's pro bono with the corporation's core business and work of other teams.

Increasingly there is an appetite from law firms to partner with their client's legal departments on international, as well as, domestic, pro bono. This can offer an easy way to become involved. Joint teams from private practice and in-house enable a broad range of skills to be drawn together. They also mean that the size of an in-house team ceases to be a constraint.

This year has seen Citi working to bring down the cost of remittances, Coca-Cola supporting entrepreneurship in Africa and Microsoft offering new innovation centres in Morocco, Nigeria, Rwanda and Africa. Lawyers meanwhile are equally involved. Through assisting in the restructuring of global NGOs, offering training on Alternative Dispute Resolution and partnering with government to manage and maintain legal aid systems, progress is being made. However, with four billion in global "legal" need, the demand for assistance and the impact of involvement is exceptionally great. ●

To find out more about participating in international pro bono efforts, the following contacts may be helpful:

Advocates for International Development – www.a4id.org

Cyrus Vance Centre for International Justice – www.abcny.org/VanceCenter.index.htm

International Bar Association – www.internationalprobono.com

International Senior Lawyers Project – www.islp.org

PILI – www.pili.org

Sources:

[1]Commission on the Legal Empowerment of the Poor, "Making the Law Work for Everyone," June 2008, p3

[2] Kemal Dervis, United Nations Development Programme Administrator, Business Call to Action, 6th May 2008

14.
Moving the Global Law Firm Through a Challenging Economy: Focus on Strategy

Jolene Overbeck (l), Chief Marketing Officer
DLA Piper, New York
and Mary K Young, Partner (r)
Zeughauser Group, Washington DC

L aw firms with teams of lawyers on different continents have platforms that work well for the world's global companies. They can expand into new markets as their clients expand and they can add to practice capabilities as their clients' needs change. However, recent economic events mean that global law firms will have to adapt more quickly than ever. Clients' needs are changing at an unprecedented pace because their companies face extraordinary challenges leading to declining revenues and narrowing margins.

Global law firms will add value if they can stay on top of the rapid pace of change and adapt along with their clients. However, the pressure that their clients are under will translate into rate pressure and lower demand for many practice areas. Global firms are better positioned to withstand economic pressures because they are diversified across markets and practices. As a result, they will have more economic power to react to opportunities. On the other hand, it is more difficult for global firms to change quickly. A strategic plan is a very helpful tool to guide any law firm through the decisions it faces. For global firms it is essential because their challenges and opportunities have many more dimensions: more markets, more clients, more talent, more leaders and more practices.

The Role of the Strategic Plan

Global firms that have a clear, focused and detailed strategy in place will be best suited to meet challenges and leverage opportunities. Most firms' strategic plans give them general guidance regarding their vision, values and growth strategies. However the true test of a strategic plan's value lies in its ability to guide the firm through challenging economic times. The strategic plan must include comprehensive goals with plans for implementing them that are specific enough to help the firm determine what to do and what not to do when faced with extraordinary threats and opportunities.

At its essence, strategic planning is about making choices, including:

- Where and how to grow

- What markets in which to compete

- How to improve profitability

- Which clients are most valuable and how to strengthen those relationships

- What kind of talent is necessary to meet firm goals and how best to attract and retain that talent

- What types of leadership and management structures are necessary to implement the firm's plans across geography, practices and functions

- How best to develop effective firm and client-team leaders

In times of economic stress, law firms will be faced with more choices than ever. Weaker firms will continue to shed lawyers and offices, and some will close their doors forever. Global firms, with their portfolios of clients, markets and practices, will be well-positioned to react to these opportunities. However, the costs of running a multi-office global firm are high and expansion is expensive. A robust strategic plan can help firms act quickly and avoid costly mistakes because it streamlines decision-making.

This is particularly true in a global firm because decision-making conducted on an ad hoc basis can be very slow. Global firms need to have input from representatives of key geographies, practice areas and client teams, but that can be cumbersome. If the strategic plan is created appropriately, involving the key constituencies across the firm, it will provide a framework for dealing with contingencies. For example, economic upheaval has brought about many opportunities to recruit individuals and small groups of laterals. Strong strategic plans will provide guidelines and procedures for determining which of these opportunities to pursue and how to pursue them without engaging in extensive new discussions across the firm.

Start From a Set of Assumptions

A strategic plan is based on a set of assumptions about the firm. These include the strengths (internal), weaknesses (internal), opportunities (external), and threats (external) that the firm must deal with, factors such as:

- Core capabilities
- Competitive advantages
- Competitive threats
- Diversity and strength of client base
- Market share in markets, sectors and practices
- Brand strength
- Market and industry trends

In times of rapid change, many of these fundamentals will change and the analysis underlying the plan will need to be revisited to reflect those changes.

To bring this process to life, firms need leaders who are in tune with the internal and external factors that have the greatest impact on their firms, know how to track and measure those factors and can react quickly when significant change occurs. In short, the plan cannot remain static; when major changes in the environment occur, the firm leadership must act immediately to revise the firm's plans as necessary. For example, we are experiencing rapid and severe changes in the financial services industry throughout the world. Global law firms that do significant business with these ailing giants and rely on the transactions they generate, should have already drawn up plans that address how to help their clients through difficult times as well as how to deal with large declines in expected revenue. Immediately thereafter, the firm must address the long-term implications of a restructured financial sector, revising the strategic plan as necessary.

What are you trying to achieve, and with whom?

The essence of a strong strategic plan is communicated in the vision statement; it articulates what the firm is striving to achieve. Fee-earners and staff should be able to communicate the vision easily. As important is the positioning statement, which articulates the firm's target market and value proposition to its external audiences. It must be consonant with the vision. The positioning statement defines the firm's highest priority markets.

In defining the market, it is best to be as specific as possible, defining geography, size, industry and services provided. In addition it articulates how the firm benefits its markets vs. competition. For example, "We are the firm of choice for the most important cross-border transactions conducted by the world's largest multinational corporations because we have the largest and best integrated team of experienced corporate lawyers in each of the critical jurisdictions around the world."

The positioning statement brings the strategy to life because it is used to guide all of the firm's marketing and business development activities. When appropriately and consistently implemented, along with the visual identity—name, logo and graphics—it helps the firm build the brand it wishes to achieve in the marketplace, and is, therefore, critical to achieving its strategy.

Focus on Profitability and Client Satisfaction

The firm's strategy should include a plan to improve the fundamental operational drivers of profitability: productivity, realization, collections, expense management, and rates. If the firm does not exceed industry averages among peer firms for these components, the firm will be less able to withstand the uncertainties of difficult economic times. The management tools to implement better financial practices are readily available; they just take discipline. Improvements in these areas will help insulate law firms from revenue declines and often benefit clients at the same time. For example, in-house lawyers prefer timely bills because it helps them manage their budgets.

Ensuring that rates are comparable to peer firms is an important driver of profitability. Firms continue to raise rates in spite of the recession. That said, great care needs to be taken in these times. Rate increases are trending lower than in previous years and there will be more push-back from cash-strapped clients. Law firms need to be sensitive to their clients' situations and be creative about alternative arrangements.

After many years of discussion, the momentum appears to be shifting towards alternative pricing. For example, some leaders of large law firms report that they are entering into an increasing number of fixed-fee arrangements in litigation matters while a portion of transactional matters, which are often easier to predict, have been billed that way for some time. These pricing arrangements may involve risk-sharing, allowing the law firm to share in the gains if a matter settles early. Clients are looking for predictability regarding rates, not necessarily lower rates. Firms that can manage litigation so that costs are predictable will be well-positioned to benefit from this trend. With regard to collections, clients will be paying more slowly. If collection practices have not already been optimized, changes should be implemented now. It is not only beneficial for the law firm, but for client as well, since timely bills enable them to better manage their budgets.

Staying Close to the Client

Any viable law firm strategic plan includes a marketing and business development section. The firm should continue to implement that plan during an economic downturn. Of first importance on this front is building and maintaining profitable, long-term client relationships, particularly for global law firms, which span or have the potential to span multiple jurisdictions.

The starting point is to have a clear view of the clients the firm represents and those it aspires to represent. Winnowing the base to eliminate unprofitable clients and in tandem developing a keen understanding of the top clients' requirements and preferences are the next steps. Firms may be reluctant to eliminate any client relationship in tough times, but making sure that the firm's clients are profitable is just sound business management. The firm needs to focus precious resource on clients that are profitable or that have the potential to be more profitable if the firm builds the relationship. Staying in close contact with those clients then protects the firm's most critical asset.

Regular client relationship status meetings are one of the best ways to help ensure a strong partnership with the firm's clients and to gain clarity about how best to support the client's business. They are not easy to implement but this is a great time to start if such meetings are not already in place. Corporate legal departments are eager to meet with their law firms to determine how those firms can help them navigate difficult times and changing environments. Global client teams can also be developed to organize a firm's efforts with respect to key clients. Global teams not only help build institutional relationships, they also allow the law firm to efficiently leverage the insights its professionals have on the client's behalf around the world. These teams have the added value of enhancing bonding and collegiality among lawyers from many cultures as they work together on client matters.

The client base analysis and regular client meetings will help clarify which markets or practices to expand or curtail. This will in turn enable the firm to make the right choices about what kind of lawyers and how many it needs in a particular geographic region to meet client requirements. Salaries and rent are the largest expense items for law firms and managing those numbers carefully is perhaps the most critical element of surviving a downturn in a way that does not damage the firm's ability to serve clients or undermine its strategy.

Conclusions

Armed with a strong strategic plan, the firms that identify the trends and move on them first will benefit greatly. The first few firms to enter a particular market or practice area will almost always achieve a much larger market share than later entrants. The classic example is Skadden, which was one of the earliest firms to understand and serve clients in the hostile takeover market as it developed. The traditional M&A firms entered much later and Skadden became a powerhouse in M&A as a result.

We live in unpredictable times, and law firms should be prepared for changes as

- The focus of litigation changes in reaction to market turmoil

- Capital flows again and new investment vehicles or M&A tools are created

- National governments and world bodies pass new laws and add regulations to correct for past market excesses

- Climate change and demand for clean energy drive energy investment

Firms should leverage those trends that are consonant with its vision and strategies and resist the opportunities that do not leverage existing strengths. Firms that focus where they have the basics in place will be able to ride the trends to success. Clients need lawyers who can help them make sense of the new landscape, find new opportunities, and protect them against new and more pervasive threats. If the firm can add value to its clients when times are tough, it will be well-positioned for new work as the recovery begins. ●

15.
Implementing Fundamental Change in a Global Law Firm

Paul Smith
Partner
Eversheds LLP, London

E. Leigh Dance interviewed Paul Smith.

Long before it was fashionable, you had a vision that your firm could serve corporate clients from many countries across many jurisdictions. Where did you start?
When I joined the embryonic Eversheds back in 1987, I remember going to my first international partners meeting, which was four guys in a room at a conference hotel. From that moment, I believed we could become an international player. I had come over from Freshfields and I just wanted to be an international lawyer.

The changes really started with our client care program and targeting US clients with UK subsidiaries. In the early 90's, we started to realize that there was more to the relationship than simply doing the work and counting the hours. About the same time we had begun actively developing US clients through referrals from US law firms. One of the referral firms was going through a painful Request for Proposal (RFP) process with DuPont, where the number of firms was reduced from 460 to 30. That was the first inkling I had of convergence. DuPont came at a crucial moment when we decided we might be better off going directly to the clients. At a firm retreat, we concluded that the UK subsidiaries of US companies didn't necessarily have the power to instruct local lawyers. So we identified their US General Counsel and went to visit them. That was a crucial step.

How did Eversheds win DuPont?

When we started to target US clients, we had sessions to develop our messages and approach. We had a role play on selling the messages to US in-house counsel, and the most unlikely partner turned out to be amazingly good. When we learned that he had sales training in another career, we embarked on sales training. Eventually most of our lawyers went through the Spin Selling program, and it gave us useful skills to develop transatlantic clients. Lawyers are terrible at listening; they want to constantly talk and offer solutions. Spin Selling teaches you to listen and ask probing questions.

But we also won DuPont for our legal skills. DuPont chose three firms, and two were incumbents. We had never done any work for them before, and they loved our pitch, but the primary reason was not our client care or US focus. It was our strength in environment, health and safety—a practice I developed and headed at the firm.

What happened after the DuPont work in Europe came in 1996?

DuPont's model came with a lot of operating structure. They required sharing knowledge with other firms, higher standards of reporting and more sophisticated billing. It really forced us to up our game. In the early days with DuPont, the real learning curve was getting internal resource to actually do the reporting, the billing, the finance, as opposed to simply doing the legal work and sending a bill. We had to build a management capability in the firm that we previously hadn't had.

Did the reporting and billing approaches cross practices?

It covered everything. The shock wave with DuPont—and it's seen somewhat as part of our firm's history—came at the start, when DuPont instructed us on a $3 billion acquisition. We had never done anything of that magnitude. It was covered in the legal media and drew resentment from some other firms. One Magic Circle partner actually called DuPont's General Counsel in the US to complain that Eversheds shouldn't be doing work like this. That was a nice motivator for us.

For you, the DuPont instruction provided a perfect way to gain internal power to push further change, right?

Yes. That DuPont acquisition was a huge job for what was then a collection of regional offices and a small London office, all operating fairly independently. Coincidentally we got another monster multi-million deal from another client that week. We suddenly had 20 lawyers working on two transactions. The logistics and the organization really tested us, and we came through. DuPont were delighted with what we had achieved, and the fees were substantially below what they would have paid to the Magic Circle, so it was a win-win. And it really kick-started our first major international client relationship.

It is often said that law firms are remarkably immune to changing their business model with the times. Why do you think that's the case?

By and large, not enough law firms have felt the pressure to change. We changed our model for two reasons: 1) we wanted to serve more international clients and so we knew we had to really understand and meet their overall needs, and 2) because a particular client was very demanding—for the legal skill, the delivery approach and the metrics to support it. Tyco and DuPont have insisted that we bring in new approaches and systems. Few clients have that vision and make clear demands on their outside counsel. For us, the client is the catalyst.

What was the next step on your journey?

I came back from a meeting with DuPont's partner law firms where we were presented early case assessment as a project management approach, and told my partner John Heaps about it. DuPont showed how you could apply these principles to litigation, a practice John headed. A light went on for both of us and we began training all litigators to do early case assessments. That led 10 years later to the launch of Rapid, an approach our litigators now use across our global network to reach a resolution that's right for the client. We applied similar methodology in the M&A practice which our lawyers use across our offices to take a consistent project management approach to corporate transactions.

How has DuPont gotten law firms to use its methodology, while so many companies complain that law firms aren't listening?

I think Tom Sager, now General Counsel, has been a strong leader throughout all this. And many of the engagement partners, like me, have been there since the beginning. We are all very passionate about the model, not only in terms of working for DuPont, but also for the opportunities it has created for us.

In the States, starting from around 2001, I used to hear from corporate counsel in the US: "Those lawyers at Eversheds, they get it." How did you pull that off?

I think we actually went out and listened to what clients wanted and of course all the DuPont work gave us a story to tell. And our sales skill training helped us to get our messages across more clearly.

This seems so straightforward—so why don't more firms go this route?

It was controversial for others. While we were getting all this publicity for DuPont, there was a small chorus against us. A top global in-house lawyer said, "I don't believe in partnering. It's not the firm—I want the best lawyers on my work, no matter the cost." I remember speaking with Tom Sager at a conference in Monte Carlo, and a lot of partners in the audience said, "Why on earth would a firm commit to do all these things?" But I think history proved us right. We now have hundreds of major US clients.

How do you maintain the pace of change as new lawyers and laterals come on board and you open new offices?

Internally, big wins and publicity are a huge help. In the early days of

DuPont we had some nonsense with Eversheds' regional offices. Each region's PR department independently sent a press release saying the Newcastle office of Eversheds acted on a $3 billion acquisition for ICI, or the Norwich office acted on a $3 billion acquisition. We had to convince the partnership that it was inefficient and we didn't look like one merged firm.

Serving DuPont and other clients we won in the US gave our offices the experience of working together. It was a very powerful example of what could be achieved, and confirmed that we were far better as one firm than as separate units. Everyone understood that the massive DuPont win brought big transactions to offices that might have previously been seen as small-scale domestic operations. That fuelled further international expansion.

How did Europe come into the mix?

Often one initiative sparks another. In this case, while implementing our client relationship management (CRM) program, we realized that many UK clients needed us across Europe. It was a tipping point—initially we assumed that a company's in-house counsel in their Newcastle headquarters would choose outside lawyers to use in Birmingham or London. Suddenly we saw that companies were organizing themselves on bigger geographies, such as Europe, Middle East and Africa (EMEA), and that their decision makers might actually be in Brussels or Munich or Madrid. It sounds so obvious in retrospect. We first expanded into western Europe, and eventually our network grew to a critical mass. Guided by our Chairman Alan Jenkins, we added Central and Eastern Europe, then Shanghai, and last year the Gulf and with Tyco, South Africa.

Did everyone buy in? I can't imagine all of your lawyers in the UK had these pan-European clients and multi-jurisdiction work.

In fact there was a very tough period when firm management was not convinced. While some of us were out banging the international drum, it was a very big leap for a predominantly UK firm with UK clients to go global. It was expensive and time consuming and felt risky. I felt a bit out on a limb at times—we would gather together our "European Enthusiasts," a core of 30 or so people who kept the spirit of international alive. Behind the scenes there was a lot of debate on the future firm strategy. I had to exercise a lot of patience as the firm collectively went through the angst.

I don't think you can overestimate how hard that sort of change really is, and then Tyco arrived to give a big push.

There's nothing like the power of a promising client to inspire change in a law firm. Whilst we were doing work for other clients on a pan-European basis, the scale of the Tyco project was enormous. It took five years to take our first meeting with Tyco to an ultimate appointment. We have an agreement with Tyco, in its third year, as the sole law firm providing legal services for about 80% of its work across 37 jurisdictions in EMEA. It's a job that 280 law firms used to do.

Winning Tyco was another huge tipping point, and the publicity and awards related to it have helped us both internally and externally. It differentiates us from other firms and it is confirmation of the global opportunity. We have learned a lot through the Tyco relationship. And since clients are increasingly demanding transparency and predictability on costs, they see and refer to us as the vanguard.

While you were competing for Tyco, you spent time with global corporate heads of legal, helping them with the structure and approach to use outside counsel effectively internationally. Where did you find time to do all this?

Eventually I didn't. I had started our regulatory practice, and am still heading one of the leading environmental, health and safety (EHS) practices in the country. That and massive time developing US clients and pan-European business development got to be too much. The firm decided to focus on my strength in building international client relationships. So I backed off the regulatory practice and got more back-up for the EHS practice.

Eversheds puts a lot of talent and resource into the client support infrastructure and management. It's a big part of your global offering and a missing link for many firms. How do you do it?

We concluded ten years ago that it merits the investment. We are very different to a US law firm in the way we share profit—rather than eat what you kill, it's divided up according to your value to the business.

That creates flexibility. Our US focus made us broaden our approach early on, to service the whole. Broadening the relationship across many offices requires management, and each engagement partner sees that as a responsibility.

For example, you have a global account management system used with Tyco and now others. How does that get paid for?

We made an enormous initial investment in that system as part of our Tyco work, with a realization that we could apply it for other multi-jurisdictional clients. We now have proof—we've developed, tested and delivered information and legal support across 37 jurisdictions for one client. The system is a powerful differentiator for clients.

It must take lots of stamina pushing major change in a global firm.

There were ups and downs, but mostly ups. In a way, it all came together last year when I won *Lawyer of the Year* at the Legal Business Awards. It was really based on my work with corporate counsel including Tyco and DuPont, and it was wholly unexpected. You were there, you saw how surprised I was. I'm sitting there with hundreds of senior partners of international law firms and then they call out my name and say that I am the *Lawyer of the Year*, the ultimate accolade. I am proud to be a lawyer, and I like being a lawyer at Eversheds.

What's the next stage of global client demand?

Corporations are retrenching in many places but there is also growth in emerging markets. They need legal services coverage, so we often manage remote firms on the client's behalf. As opposed to the client going cold to find advisors for a new matter in Turkey or Kazakhstan, for example, we find the firm and have their work managed and billed in a consistent way. We can now bill all these countries with one bill in US dollars and feed it into a US electronic management system.

Can smaller law departments with smaller budgets use these tools?

Small law departments just as often need advice in foreign markets, and we focus on the clearest path to getting the right firm for them. We offer a one-stop solution to finding lawyers in other countries and managing them on our client's behalf in a consistent way. For a lot of these lawyers and firms now, Eversheds is the client because we represent many major multinational clients. We have well-established relationships and the buying power to get the right level of service and commitment. It's a compelling client benefit.

What's the next big challenge?
The world economy. I don't know where we are going with all this. History tells us that you do eventually come out the other side, but I think the world will look very different in terms of the balance of power between various countries and the fact that there will be far greater regulation of business. We'll see, right? ●

16.
The Fulfilled International Lawyer:
Advice for a Successful Career

John H. Stout
Partner
Fredrikson & Byron, Minneapolis

The places your kids take you can change your life. My appreciation for the many benefits of an international, personal and business life has its roots in my two children's early fascination with China. Both started studying Chinese when they were 13. My early visits to China (1987, 1992) were to chaperone a high school trip to seven cities, visit both children as they took college years of study in Beijing, and later to visit one while he lived in Beijing for two years following graduation. My world expanded; my appreciation of Asian culture developed; my sense of global interconnectedness and world citizenship increased dramatically.

Speaking of life-changing events, look at the developments of the last year. It's a particularly thought-provoking time to reflect on an international legal practice; its satisfactions and challenges. Globalization has deep roots going back a couple of thousand years. But the globalization of finance and commerce, accompanied by the globalization of the rule of law, has accelerated dramatically in the last few decades. This acceleration has been facilitated by liberalizing political attitudes towards free trade, the expansion into global markets by transnational enterprises, international finance and credit facilitation, globalizing governance and business principles, the emergence of English as the international language of commerce and the facilitation of communication by the Internet.

In the early 1990's as the Marketing Partner of a relatively small firm (100 lawyers at the time, 240 now) I began to think about how what I saw in the world might impact the practice of law in Minneapolis. I was happily dividing my time between securities law, entertainment law and directors' and officers' responsibility (an early version of corporate governance) practices.

Mono-lingual White Male was Not the Prototype

My initial observation back then was that some of our smallest corporate clients were beginning to do business in international markets. My second observation was that it would be increasingly important to client retention and development to have international service skills to meet the needs of these clients directly. I felt networks would be useful as a supplement but not as a substitute for needed skills. My third observation was that a mono-lingual white male like me, with international interests and exposure, was not the prototype for developing the firm's international capabilities. Culture and language, in addition to intelligence and an excellent legal education, often procured in multiple jurisdictions, would be key.

It's no accident that during this formative period, Leigh Dance was the firm's Head of Marketing, bringing her experience and passion for international business to us and our clients. Today, that passion and vision continues to be realized in a firm which now speaks 16 languages, has attorneys cross-licensed from Europe, Asia and Mexico, and serves hundreds of clients doing business on all of the world's continents.

I chaired Fredrikson's International Law practice for many years, and was a consistent champion (or pain, depending on which partner you ask) when it came to devoting resources to broadening our firm's cultural fabric and geographic interests. As global markets developed, it became more and more apparent that clients needed us to help them achieve their international objectives. Talented associates and laterals joining our firm appreciated our international focus and the cultural diversity we embraced. As for me, it all goes back to the influence of my kids. I simply wanted to work at a place where I could live globalization first-hand. I wanted to be able to stay connected to my clients and address their issues (with the help of locally qualified lawyers) no matter where they were doing business.

Living Globalization First-hand

While developing the firm's international capabilities and my own international practice, I've had some tremendously rewarding experiences. My career has taken me to many countries in the last decade, including Dubai, Oman, Tunisia, Cyprus, China, Thailand, South Africa, France, Italy and the UK in the last two years. Among the memorable experiences that have expanded my horizons and led me to be a better lawyer are:

• Serving as a director of the Center for International Private Enterprise, Washington, DC (CIPE). CIPE is a non-profit corporation funded by U.S. Agency for International Development and The Foundation for Democracy. It works through local organizations to promote private enterprise and democratic principles around the world, including in some of the most challenging countries (Iraq and Afghanistan, to name two). CIPE uses corporate governance as one of the major means to carry out its mission. With CIPE I've made governance presentations in several countries including Tunisia and recently Oman.

• Serving as the Vice Chair of the American Bar Association's Corporate Governance Committee and Co-chair of its International Governance Developments Subcommittee, a wonderful opportunity for exchange with attorneys throughout the world, for which I recently moderated an Internet-supported conference call with 50 participants from many international jurisdictions and seven presenters, on the impact of the worldwide financial crisis in their respective countries.

• Membership in the International Corporate Governance Network, an organization which serves the world's largest investment funds (e.g. CalPers and TIAA-Cref from the US as well as other international institutional investors).

• Membership in the National Association of Corporate Directors (NACD) which provides education for, and facilitates interaction among, directors of companies doing business worldwide. I have had several leadership roles in NACD and worked with and given presentations to corporate directors in the US, Jordan, UK and the Netherlands, and assisted NACD in forming the Global Directors Development Circle, a seven-country group of organizations with missions similar to that of NACD.

• Membership in the Caux Roundtable, an organization formed by business leaders from Japan, Europe and the United States to develop and promote principles of ethical business conduct in the various societies in which business is conducted. Caux hosts annual conferences internationally, the most recent of which dealt with the subject of moral capitalism.

Some of these activities I got involved in partly for business development reasons, to meet potential clients and get closer to the key issues facing my practice. Other times I participated as a curious learner.

To me, a fulfilled international lawyer is committed to what he or she does, valued by his or her clients for the international experience and perspectives, and fueled by the changing array of global influences. For me, satisfaction is being part of the process; satisfaction is working with domestic businesses succeeding in diverse global markets, and working with companies from other markets as they do business in the US. It is extraordinary to feel the sense of global citizenship that comes with forging relationships with colleagues worldwide, honor the differences among the many cultures one encounters, and enjoy discovering so many shared values and views. Challenges? No question. Opportunities? Always. Change? The only constant in this rapidly evolving world. ●

17.
Changing Supply and Demand for Global Legal Services: The Multi-polar Dynamic

David Syed
Senior Partner – Europe, Orrick, Paris

E. Leigh Dance interviewed David Syed of Orrick.

What are the big changes right now in global demands for legal services?

Lots of change is happening simultaneously, and much of it is an acceleration of trends that have been around for more than 20 years. Globalization, segmentation, and consolidation are just clearer and clearer. If anything, the current financial crisis will further accelerate those trends by subtracting legal demand and reducing legal spend. This will introduce greater efficiency into the market. Efficiency has already started, with more information available than ever before to clients. Law firms are now more corporate; it's easy to know partners' revenues, to understand the rate structures of firms. These efficiencies result from elasticity of demand; they weren't available 20 to 25 years ago when law firms were opaque back offices. Now clients have more information about how to use law firms most efficiently as a factor in their own costs of production. These efficiency trends will accelerate.

The new factors influencing global legal services demand are linked to geopolitical changes and the shifting balance of economic power in the world. We are beginning to see a new world emerge from the effects of globalization and the results of the financial crisis.

I see the financial crisis as the end result of a series of trends that have been in place for a long time, related to where value is being created in the world. There are a whole range of things happening simultaneously in places like China, Silicon Valley, and the Middle East which is causing these markets to be much more prominent in the world markets because of the value that is being created there. As a result, we are seeing the emergence of a much more multi-polar world, which means we need a much more multi-polar legal organization to service that multi-polar world.

The top 50 law firms in the world are generally not looking at regions and cities; we are looking at world markets. There has been a paradigm shift in the way we have to structure and organize to serve the multi-polar world. It encompasses how we train lawyers, what legal service we give, what law, what language, where we put our resources, how we bill and collect, how we assess profitability and performance... it really impacts the whole spectrum of a law firm's activities. The yard stick that we would use to measure a more centric system no longer works.

Is this really the way the top 50 firms in the world are managing, with leadership looking to change the spectrum of what they do to respond to a multi-polar world?

Some firms are getting there faster than others. I see two very different management approaches. There are the global firms that have been playing internationally from a certain market or a central base. Firms with a New York or London origin are classic examples: the center is still driving them. A global firm from Paris, for example, will have developed an international strategy from a French base. Their mindset and DNA reflects that center, from culture to finance. If the firm is driving clients from the center out, the management will not likely be multi-polar. In those cases growth is often tied to a fundamental contract between the center and the outpost, i.e., the office—and the center generates and controls much of the approach to the work and the client relationships.

The other approach is being followed in firms like Orrick, where I do think the management is changing rapidly for this multi-polar world. These firms have a more deterministic strategy—they propel themselves in the direction they want to go from no specific origin. Latham and Sidley are examples of this approach; they are not defined by their headquarters either financially or operationally. These firms tend to develop by aggregating businesses across the world that make sense, to produce something better than the sum of the parts. It's a completely different model, based really on necessity because these firms could not adopt the model of a Slaughter & May or a Sullivan & Cromwell, as they don't have the bases to do it.

This other approach also creates a self-fulfilling, virtuous circle. At Orrick we have people that appreciate the less-centric approach. We may go broader into certain markets than a centrally-focused service organization would. This enables us to bring more high quality people to the firm in the local markets, and thereby enhances the whole. Our people want to make a strong impact on the local market, which translates to a broader market impact for the firm as whole than a centralized firm with a narrower focus. The end result is higher quality in individual markets. This complements the trend of global business which is becoming multi-polar as well, and so the law firms following this strategy can flex and grow to meet client needs much more effectively.

Are other private practice lawyers out there really prepared to excel in this multi-polar environment? Don't most firms still make very culturally-rooted decisions?

They are definitely still rooted, but far less so than five years ago. It's a work in progress. We talk to lateral candidates who have been in Magic Circle firms in their local markets and many really don't like it. Their opportunities and issues are often treated as remote—no matter how good they are, they find they have little influence in London. Orrick and firms like us offer a great alternative to those that don't like that command-control model. Entrepreneurial lawyers want to have an impact both in the market where they are and in the organization where they work.

With lawyers feeling empowered within various geographies and markets, how do you preserve the global brand and deliver consistent service?

It's not easy, because obviously the centrifugal tendencies are greater the more diverse you get. There can be a tendency for the markets to pull different sectors of an international firm in different directions. There is no one solution but a number of solutions, and this requires a new management emphasis for law firms.

Firms must first and foremost be dedicated to bringing people together: at the end of the day, the brand is the people. Technology and other tools facilitate and enable, but the core is our people. People within the firm must lead and connect other people, making sure that the brand as a whole is strong and prominent. The second necessity is to enable interaction and support teamwork remotely and in multiple locations through structure, technology, training and process.

This will happen more readily if the firm is truly focused on its clients. Ralph Baxter and the Orrick leadership have truly embraced this as an organizing principle—this complex machine we have built has one overarching purpose that cuts across everything we do: serving the client. If you embark on any management initiative or growth strategy that is in any way disconnected from real client relationships, you just won't get the results you need or want.

What skills do the management and leadership of Orrick need in order to succeed in this world you've described?

The skills for leadership are very different today than they were 10, 20, 30 years ago. It will take different types of people to lead and manage these firms successfully. More and more, we need to talk about management "teams" as opposed to management embodied within specific individuals or small groups of people with separate, defined responsibilities. We need individual accountability of course, but the team approach will be paramount. The issues will be diverse, complex, fast moving and hard to read, requiring a management team of people from different origins, reflecting the multi-polar nature of the organization and the issues that come up in managing a large, far-flung professional services organization. Management needs to be representative of the component parts while also being responsible for the whole. Following the lead of global business, management within home country and outside home country must be fully integrated.

It's a nice idea, but don't you find that the idea of making the firm's headquarters or domestic offices truly global in perspective is a long way off?

It's about truly having the whole world's perspective being represented wherever you are, and that is very difficult, I think. It's difficult anywhere there is a dominant culture—Paris or London come to mind—but the increase in truly global companies is leading us there. Take the example of the oil companies, who are truly global, non-centric, and de-localized and have been that way for decades. Their in-house law departments are an amazing cultural array of expertise. The lawyers are Malaysian, Pakistani, Emiratis, English, American, Australian and everything in between, and they all move all over. There is no locus. It's not because you're English you'll be in London, you might be in Dubai. Eventually as global firms we need to reach that level of global diversity, with each of our offices having a truly global perspective.

So what about coverage: how many locations or geographies is enough?

We are going into a buyer's market for at least the next couple of years, and the client will again be at the center of the response to that question. Where do they want people? I suggest what I call sub-regional hubs. We take the current regional model of firms to another level. Emerging markets are often sub-regions in their own right: Dubai and the Middle-East is a sub-regional market. Another example is Warsaw, which could be a sub-regional hub for all of the Baltics and Ukraine, which in themselves are too small. I think we can expect the same for Africa as it becomes a more serious, active participant in global commerce. There might be a North-Africa hub and a South-Africa hub.

I like the sub-regional concept because it is a healthy compromise between being everywhere like Baker & McKenzie or a White & Case and being concentrated in a few regional markets like London or New York. Locating everywhere makes it very difficult to maintain the culture and integrity of legal service. On the other hand, firms located just in major financial and commercial centers can't go where the clients are growing their businesses, where they need coverage.

We're not just talking about the BRIC countries. Goldman Sach's recent report talks about the next 11 fast growth markets – Bangladesh, Egypt, Indonesia, Iran, South Korea, Mexico, Nigeria, Pakistan, Philippines, Turkey and Vietnam. We're clearly not going to set up offices in all those countries tomorrow morning, but we could set up regional hubs which will allow us to get close enough to those markets and offer better coverage to our clients than our competitors.

The distinction between practices isn't nearly as clean as law firms have practiced it in the US and the UK. Do you see the approach to distinctive practices changing in the future?
The trend in legal practice has been from generalist to specialist, and then from specialist to global specialist. Now I would characterize the trend as moving from global specialist to global synthesis. What clients are looking for is a synthesis in the sense of bringing knowledge and advice together and packaging them to give a global solution which brings into play both regional specialties, client specialties, industry expertise, legal practice specialties, and institutional experience. They don't care about distinct legal areas of practice per se.

The know-how management part of this is very important, and the problem is the building blocks. You need to track all your English-language data, your French-language data, and things are going so fast that we don't track the know-how very well. We do need to bring together these elements and train lawyers in this approach. Perhaps it's a new talent model that firms are beginning to develop the lawyer who can't communicate with the client and bring everything together. They may have a practice specialty of their own, but fundamentally they are managing client relationships and proposing solutions, assembling the best advice the firm has to offer from its many component parts, synthesizing it in a coherent way and integrating it with the client's business goals.

If the client has a big dispute somewhere, it could lead to a restructuring, to a sale, to arbitration—in the same market or elsewhere. A good lawyer will integrate these issues on behalf of the client. You need corporate, security litigation, regulatory, arbitration, and you have umpteen different countries. If we want to play at the top level we need people who can bring all that together on the client's behalf. This is why, as I've said before, we need groups of people with a diversified perspective and who are focused on global clients and ongoing training in putting the know-how in place to enable that type of thought and service to emerge in firms. Very few firms have this today.

What's the latest dynamic that presents an opportunity for law firms?

The financial crisis actually opens up lots of new markets to law firms. Today, the ethical constraints of lawyers, which have been a hindrance in the past, will be more valued by clients. When we look at what the investment banks have been doing for the last 10-20 years—giving all sorts of advice to clients with very little confidentiality, no real liability attached to it, a minimal code of ethics other than self-governance, a range of inherent conflicts of interest—and we see where that has gotten us: to trillions of dollars of losses. So law firms are in fact ideally suited to a certain type of advisory service to clients—especially if they can bring together this idea of synthesized globally oriented, commercially focused legal advice, which they have not been too good at in the past. I think there may be a whole new market out there that we don't fully recognize yet. The question is who will occupy it? Maybe the accounting firms, maybe boutique investment banks that set up independent funded global networks, but I don't see why law firms can't be part of the solution. ●

18.
Lawyers Network Differently as the World Grows Flatter

Derek Benton
Director – International Operations
LexisNexis Martindale-Hubbell, London

As someone who has spent the last 25 years travelling the globe in my role with Martindale-Hubbell, I have spent countless hours networking with in-house and outside counsel of all shape, sizes, nationalities and cultures. I am not alone: networking has been an essential element of professional practice since time immemorial. As business and legal practice becomes ever more global and commercial pressures have shaped the law business, we can differentiate three distinct periods in professional networking: pre-internet, early internet and now, Web 2.0.

Before the internet, international conferences and traditional printed directories were significant ways to connect with other lawyers, partly because they were more efficient, and also because rules on ethics and various restrictions prevented more overt methods of networking. Although notionally educational events, much of the business of international conferences was about collecting as many business cards as possible. Once back at the office, participants would use directories such as Martindale-Hubbell to establish whether or not the pleasant chap from Tuesday's tea break worked for a firm that they'd genuinely consider instructing.

If the conferences failed to serve up a lawyer from a specific country they were interested in, networking was more haphazard. Pouring through legal directories, clients would base their decisions on a few hundred words of the firm's own promotional material, plus the views of any of their colleagues who had vaguely heard of them. This was not a rigorous, scientific endeavour.

During the early phase of the internet, "disintermediation" was the buzz word in the legal circles I moved in. Why should law firms supply directories with their lawyers' biographies, when the same information could be posted free of charge on their own website? To which the obvious answer was: How do you think that anyone is going to find your website, among the millions of others? Some legal directories also pointed out that client feedback was their unique selling point. It's all very well having your own website, but if clients aren't offered an independent opinion of that firm's performance, how does your own website help win instructions?

During this 1990s "stand-off" phase, a completely random idea dreamed up in a West London house set the scene for what we now know as Web 2.0. Friends Reunited was a simple concept—allowing former classmates to read about each other, and re-establish contact. It was a spectacular success—and was even said to be responsible for a spate of divorces, as old flames re-established contact. But like its spiritual successors of MySpace, Bebo and Facebook, it was a purely social tool. It did not offer the possibility of sophisticated professional networking.

Then LinkedIn was launched in 2003. Unashamedly aimed at business and professional networking, LinkedIn had a specific USP. Participants could develop their own personal networks based around professional recommendations—delivered online—and also mutual acquaintances. It has proved phenomenally popular, and is now regarded as a genuine tool for professionals to develop their careers and win new business.

Elsewhere in the legal market, traditional network in the form of listings directories have taken the rise of Web 2.0 to heart. They realise that it is no longer sufficient to simply aggregate listing data on their chosen markets. Potential clients increasingly expect user feedback on listed products—whether they relate to hotels, restaurants or online retailers. Especially in today's difficult economic climate, potential clients want to be assured they will receive an excellent service before parting with their hard-earned cash.

At Martindale-Hubbell we have been monitoring these developments closely. Following hundreds of hours of gathering and analyzing market feedback, we believe that buyers of legal services around the world are responsive to new ways of evaluating lawyers and firms' services, ways which will make online networking and its business development potential a reality. Leveraging our large database of law firms and lawyers' biographies, we can make online networking effective for anyone from the first day of joining. We're calling this development Martindale 2.0, and we see it as a truly radical departure for us.

My appreciation of the value of networking around the world has grown dramatically in nearly nine years of working with Leigh Dance and hundreds of in-house counsel to produce the Counsel to Counsel programme. We've gathered corporate counsel and private practice lawyers around a table in more than 60 cities and 20 countries to trade best practices and network. The in-person contact is tremendous, but the demands on our time and resources lead us to seek additional, efficient and focused ways to connect more frequently.

Like LinkedIn, the new Martindale-Hubbell Connected service will allow lawyers to identify and make contact with potentially hundreds of professionals around the world. The contacts that Connected suggests will always be based on shared experiences, whether that is common universities, previous employers, specific geographies, or even mutual acquaintances.

The preliminary results have been phenomenal. Of the circa one million lawyers listed on our database, the system has suggested millions of possible connections—on average ten for every lawyer listed. That's surely a better average than one could get at Tuesday's tea break.

Of course, in the future, international conferences will still play a vital part in professional networking. Personal chemistry is still the all-important factor in any business relationship. But Web 2.0 will allow such conferences to be used very differently in the future. And, hopefully, more effectively than ever before.

During conference sessions, participants can genuinely relax and take the time to really learn and reflect on what's being said. But how they behave during the breaks will be very different in the future. I imagine there will be far fewer conversations with random strangers and far more networking with specific individuals. For the first time, you'll be able to meet new professional contacts you've previously only ever communicated with online, to establish whether you have the personal chemistry to build a lasting working relationship.

Going forward the legal profession will increasingly want higher levels of privacy online than existing social networking sites offer. There too will be a demand for posting "user generated content" that will require confidentiality and restricted access. A trusted network of peers, online, will be an essential resource for the busy practitioner in their everyday needs of having opinions, expertise and valued counsel from colleagues. It is exciting to rise to the challenge of bringing Web 2.0 to the lawyers worldwide and personally see how far we've travelled in professional networking. ●

19.
Corporate Europe Must Improve Compliance

E. Leigh Dance and Bruno Cova

Reprinted with permission from

Financial Times, 26 May 2008

European companies are adapting too slowly to the regulatory environment, potentially giving an advantage to US corporations. The tough enforcement climate now facing European companies is nothing new in the US. It has been 30 years since its Foreign Corrupt Practices Act made the payment of foreign bribes illegal (vs. less than nine for Europe). The so-called "long arm" of US law and years of coping with hostile legal and political environments has driven American corporations to build compliance programmes that are stronger and more far-reaching than their European counterparts.

The problems facing Siemens, the German industrial group, exemplify the cost and distraction that bog down a company suspected of wrongdoing. More than $2bn of suspicious transactions in more than 60 countries have been identified. On the legal front alone, more than €240m has been paid out in fines and penalties, with a further €474m spent on advisers. Siemens has been barred from being a supplier to the Italian, Nigerian and Norwegian governments. Top executives have resigned or been fired and several Siemens managers and consultants have been arrested or put under criminal investigation. The Siemens-Nokia joint venture was put on hold. Siemens' share price has suffered. We can expect other negative consequences long after the investigations finish.

European corporations operate in more complex environments than ever before, where the odds of facing a damaging compliance crisis are high. Markets and the media tend to view the accused as guilty as soon as a regulatory inquiry begins. Aggressive consumer groups, activist international investors and busy plaintiff lawyers relentlessly shadow corporations undergoing a compliance investigation.

Because of new laws and enforcement actions and co-operation among prosecutors and regulatory authorities, European companies also face far higher legal risks. New capital market laws and reformed codes of corporate governance mean more stringent internal controls and disclosure requirements. International bribery was made illegal by the 1997 Organization for Economic Co-operation and Development convention, and in some countries corporations have criminal liability. Competition laws are stronger and more rigorously enforced, with violations treated as criminal offences in countries such as the UK. Consumers and retail investors have greater protection and new legal remedies, such as class actions in France and Italy.

The risks multiply with so many European companies operating beyond their country of incorporation. Managers operating locally may be more tempted to accept requests for bribes or enter into anti-competitive agreements. Global operations require working with agents, suppliers, distributors and other third parties, and proper due diligence on these parties is often missing.

To be sure, more than a few Europe-headquartered global companies maintain sophisticated processes to support compliance, often as a result of past regulatory disputes. Akzo-Nobel and Shell are two examples. Most European companies, however, are ill equipped. Many corporate heads of legal affairs and compliance recognize the regulatory threats and the potentially disastrous consequences of alleged wrongdoing. Unfortunately, too many boards and chief executives practice avoidance, and let their companies operate at a competitive disadvantage.

We prescribe prompt action. Companies must commit sufficient resources to build the culture and infrastructure to address these challenges, including "mapping" of legal risks, internal controls, monitoring and action in response to compliance issues. Tone at the top is essential; closing one or both eyes and letting mid-level managers engage in illegal practices is no longer a viable commercial strategy.

A big component of US corporate compliance strength is the

prominence of the legal and compliance functions. The chief legal officer is often among the company's top paid executives, and has full access to the board and the resources he needs. It is no surprise that when Siemens elevated the global legal and compliance position to react better to the crisis, they hired a legal executive from General Electric. In-house lawyers need both status and access to corporate leadership in order to fulfill the duties expected of them.

European companies must also learn how to interact effectively with regulators during investigations, as well as to maintain relationships with officials as the company (and the law that regulates it) changes and grows. Addressing the issue of compliance is important to be able to compete effectively and preserve the company's reputation and value. Call your chief legal or compliance officer and get his views. Today.

Leigh Dance is President of ELD International, a consultancy to global corporate legal departments and law firms. Bruno Cova is a partner of Paul Hastings, former general counsel at Eni and Fiat and chief legal adviser in the Parmalat investigation. ●

20.
Focus: The Benefits of a Narrow Scope in the Face of Global Opportunity

Ross Fishman
CEO
Fishman Marketing, Highland Park, Illinois

In the 1991 comedy *"City Slickers,"* Curly, played by Jack Palance, a wise and wizened cowboy, offers some old-time western wisdom to Mitch Robbins (Billy Crystal), during his cattle-driving vacation:

Jack Palance: "Do you know what the secret of life is? One thing. Just *one thing.* You stick to that and everything else don't mean [anything]."

Billy Crystal: "Yeah, but what's that one thing?"

Jack Palance: "That's what you've got to figure out."

Interesting advice.

What's *your* "one thing?" What's your *firm's* "one thing?" As a leader in a law firm, that's what you have to figure out too. When someone needs a law firm that does "X," when does your firm automatically come to mind? When are you obviously one of the top-three choices?

Typically, the answer is "Never." It's not that you can't accomplish this, it's just that rarely is that our primary strategic or marketing goal.

What's your firm's Focus? Many firms have as their marketing goal to "get better known," or "get our name out there." It should be marketing *dominance*. And that's only accomplished with a singular focus on that goal.

But if your firm were to own a top spot in some practice area in some geographic market, what would it be? What's your brand? What do you stand for? What do you *aspire* to stand for?

More than a decade ago, Baker & McKenzie was *the* global law firm. If you wanted an English-speaking law firm in some far-flung city or country where you didn't have a direct connection, there weren't many options. Many clients simply looked to see whether Baker & McKenzie had an office there. They were the law firm that stood for "Global." If that's your goal, the activities that facilitate it become relatively obvious.

That was then. Today, many international firms have thousands of lawyers spread across dozens of countries and even more cities. Global networks have banded together hundreds of mid-sized, full-service law firms into a community that operates loosely like an international law firm. "Global" isn't enough any longer for Baker & McKenzie—or any other firm.

In 1997, *Forbes* magazine asked Skadden Arp's managing partner, Joel Flom, to identify his "personal hero—the person he most seeks to emulate." He selected *Richard Branson*, the pioneering leader of Virgin Group, because he taught Flom "the value of a brand." Flom became the principal architect of Skadden's underlying strategy which caused its historic rise to the world's third largest firm, with over $2 billion in annual revenue.

What was his secret? *Focus.* Identify exactly what you want to be known for, execute ruthlessly, and market the heck out of it.

How do you market a full-service law firm? Or a general commercial litigation or transactional practice? It's hard. Really hard. Why? Because your firm probably looks very similar to most of your top competitors.

Don't believe me? Here, let me write your website's home page for you:

Our firm is big and old. We offer the technical skills of a large firm and the collegial culture of a small firm. We have lots of offices. Our lawyers work as a team; we are efficient, service oriented, and partner with our clients.

We offer excellent, creative, timely, value-added, results-driven legal skills and business solutions. We are both ethnically diverse and community oriented. We represent *everyone*, from individuals to global corporations. We practice in every conceivable area from ADR to Zoning, and we are the best at every single one of them.

Here are 24 pages of alphabetical descriptions of every practice area, illustrated by globes, gavels, columns, handshakes, skylines, and grinning lawyers.

Sure it's factually accurate, but it's also true for nearly every one of your competitors. And you've given your prospects no reason to hire you instead of any other skilled full-service firm. That's not using marketing to its full advantage; that's simply burying yourself in the middle.

What's your firm's Mission or Vision Statement? Here's one prominent firm's version, selected at random:

The mission of [Borde Smorgas] is to provide superior legal representation to achieve optimal results in resolving a client's legal issues, while exercising the highest standards of professionalism.

What's their unique focus? *Doing good work?* Is that what separates them from their competition? They're *smart?*

Whenever US TV talk show host Oprah or her competitors needs a lawyer to discuss a woman's legal issue, who's the inevitable first choice? Gloria Allred. And she seems to be involved in all the major cases. She owns an entire *gender!* That's great marketing. Why does it work? *Focus.*

Allred doesn't have to be the best litigator in the US. She's not competing against every other litigator for every big case in every practice area in every geographic market, just those seeking to represent women on prominent women's issues. And how many are there in that category? Not many. *Focus.* It's the "big fish in a small pond" theory of marketing. And it works.

Of course, the larger the firm, the harder it is to find your focus—you have too many chiefs, too many chefs, too many conflicting practices and perspectives. However, you're not off the hook. Many of your most valued corporate clients are global businesses that have tackled the challenge of finding their focus.

Of course, lawyers would argue that identifying a narrow focus is easier in a hierarchical corporate environment than a partnership, or when your product is widgets, not Warrens or Wendys. Focus in a professional services firm means publicly prioritizing certain people over others.

Focus requires a level of strategic thinking, courage, commitment, and leadership that most law firms do not possess. But those few that do tend to be among the most successful – and profitable.

When a savvy General Counsel needs the leading Italian banking firm, or UK capital markets firm, or New York litigation firm, what would the short list look like? Would your firm be on it? The ones who *are* on it didn't do it by accident.

In the 1990s, Wilson Sonsini sought to become the leading law firm for high-tech companies, propelling themselves into first place in that market. O'Melveny & Myers, Kirkland & Ellis dominate in class-action defense litigation. Sullivan & Cromwell is arguably the leading M&A law firm on global deals (according to Bloomberg's global deals consummated lists). For bankruptcy and restructuring the obvious choices would include Weil Gotshal and Linklaters [check Legal 500 or PLC...].

Decide what you want to be known for. Make it narrow. Make it focused. Then make it happen. ●

21.
Feels Like 1990 All Over Again: Observations and Forecasts about Law Firm Economic Cycles

Ann Lee Gibson, Ph.D.,
Ann Lee Gibson Consulting, West Plains, Missouri

In the summer of 2008, I came down with a bad case of poison ivy that didn't respond to the slathering of lotions and potions I used to fight it. After three weeks of misery, I came up with a new hypothesis—perhaps I didn't have poison ivy after all—and scheduled a visit to our family doctor. He diagnosed an impressive case of hives. "It's caused by either an allergy or anxiety," he said. "But I don't know which it is."

I knew which it was. And that was before the stock market *really* tanked.

This Recession Reminds Me of the Early 1990s

As a consultant whose job it is to provide early warnings for law firms, I have long been aware that we are torpedoing over fast rapids. Although the water levels are different, many rocks are familiar.

This recession never felt like the one in 2001-02. It immediately reminded me of the one in the early nineties; a downturn that seemed like it would never end.

In 1991, I was the first marketing director of a law firm based in California, where the economy was suffering from many of the current recession's elements: overextended and failing banks, a continuing Savings & Loan crisis, falling real estate prices, rising unemployment, high gasoline prices, and more. The era of greed and big shoulder pads was definitely over.

In the early nineties, even without an Internet and the rapid-fire flow of information we enjoy today, it was common knowledge that firms were laying off associates and asking unprofitable partners to retire early or else. Some firms failed. Other firms, mortally weakened by the downturn, had no strength left to join the legal services rally when it finally arrived.

Although the causes and attributes of the current recession differ in many ways from the recession of the early nineties, there are similarities. Some of the most obvious are summarized in the table below for younger readers who were not in the work force then and for others who might have forgotten.

Please continue to full-page chart on page 121.

Similarities Between 1990-91 Recession and 2007-? Recession

	Early 1990s	2007 - ?
Failed financial institutions	The US savings and loan crisis produced failures of many banks and 700+ S&Ls, due to imprudent real estate and other lending practices, inadequate internal and external controls and regulation, fraud, and insider trading.	The subprime mortgage financial crisis—caused by predatory lending practices, inadequate internal and industry controls, and inadequate regulatory controls—crashed the global economy and stock markets.
Overinvestment in high-risk debt	Collapse of many junk bonds	Collapse of many asset-based securitizations
Government bailouts	The S&L bailout initially cost US taxpayers ≈ $120 billion, with an eventual net loss of $40 billion.	Bailouts and loans made to banks, insurance companies, and other industries along with homeowners will initially cost taxpayers $1 trillion+.
Government deficits	The US budget deficit's climb continued through the early 1990s; this trend reversed in 1993.	The US budget deficit's climb, begun anew in 2001, continues.
Housing prices	Prices reached an "all-time high" in 1990, then fell and took 10 years to recover.	Home prices reached an "all-time high" in 2006; prices are still falling.
Unemployment rate	The highest rate was 7.8% in 1992; the previous low was 5.0% in 1989.	Current predictions are for 8.5% or even higher by end of 2009; the previous recent low was 4.4% in 2007.
Stock market losses	Global stock markets crashed in October 1987 by 23% - 60%, then recovered slowly in subsequent years. The 1990 bear market bottomed on September 11, 1990.	As of January 2009, global equity markets have dropped 40%+ since 2007 Q3.
US wars	The first Persian Gulf War began in 1990 and ended in 1991.	Wars in Iraq and Afghanistan began in 2002; both wars continue.
Oil prices	Prices spiked and fell in 1990.	Prices spiked and fell in 2008.
Consumer confidence	In October 1990, 77% of Americans said, "The economy is getting worse."	In October 2008, 90% of Americans said, "The economy is getting worse," setting a new low record for consumer confidence.
US political changes	1992 – A Democratic president (Bill Clinton) replaced a Republican one (George H.W Bush).	2008 – A Democratic president (Barack Obama) replaced a Republican one (George W. Bush).

© 2009, Ann Lee Gibson Consulting

121

Lessons the 1990-91 Recession Offers about This One

I turned to published reports of law firms' financial performances to better understand the 1990-91 recession's impacts on firms. With 24 years of such reports available from *The American Lawyer* describing the financial results of the 100 largest US law firms, there was much to parse. Below are some observations about that earlier era and my forecasts about how large US law firms will likely perform in the current recession.

Extraordinarily strong law firm revenue increases presage recessions.

The appearance of the current recession, which most economists now agree began in late 2007, offers us an opportunity to find markers among law firm performances that indicate coming downturns.

My review of the Am Law 100 performance data shows that those years in which the Am Law 100 firms' total revenue increased by the greatest percentage (compared to the previous year's performance) were in each of the three years preceding the three recessions that have occurred since 1984. Those banner revenue increases occurred in fiscal years 1989 (17.8%), 2000 (17.0%), and 2007 (13.6%).

Apparently, an economic tide that lifts law firm revenue so high cannot sustain itself. This pattern announces that a downturn is imminent, due to imbalances in the marketplaces that feed large law firms.

Recessions hurt large law firm performances for a long time.

Based on Am Law firms' performances in the early 1990s, I foresee that the current recession's impacts on large law firms, particularly on partner profitability, will be felt for three to four years for most firms and longer for others. This forecast is based on how long it took many firms to recover after the 1990-91 recession.

As noted earlier, 1989 was a banner year for Am Law firms. Eighty firms were included in the Am Law lists for all eight fiscal years 1989 through 1996. From 1990-1993, more than half of those eighty firms produced profits per partner no higher than they had enjoyed in 1989 (see Table 1 below). The second year of the recession saw even more firms failing to exceed their 1989 PPP levels. It was not until 1994—five years after the recession began—that more than half of the Am Law firms in this sample finally produced partner profits beyond their 1989 levels.

Table 1: **Years in Which Am Law 100 Firms Produced Profits Per Partner (PPP) at or below 1989 PPP Levels**

	Fiscal Years						
	1990	*1991*	*1992*	*1993*	*1994*	*1995*	*1996*
Number of Am Law 100 Firms	43	48	41	41	36	30	19
Percentage	54%	60%	51%	51%	45%	38%	24%

* These data reflect the performances of those 80 firms that were listed in *all* the Am Law 100 listings for fiscal years 1989 through 1996.

© 2009, Ann Lee Gibson Consulting

It is entirely possible that large law firms will recover faster from this current recession than from the one in 1990-91. This time around, firms appear to have more quickly pared troublesome practices and unneeded resources, actions law firm leaders were slower to take in the early 1990s. However, most firms and their partners should still prepare for multiple years of lower profits per partner.

Higher-end firms suffer longest.

Partners at firms with the highest-end practices should manage particularly downward their expectations of an early recovery. A severe recession's impacts are generally felt longer by the most profitable law firms, which rely on a stream of complex, high-value deals and, therefore, must wait longer for that level of economic activity to reappear and stabilize.

Evidence of the long-lasting effects of severe global recessions on highest-end law firms is offered by their performances during the early 1990s. After 1989, seventeen of that year's twenty most profitable US law firms failed to produce profits per partner (PPP).

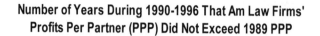

Number of Years During 1990-1996 That Am Law Firms' Profits Per Partner (PPP) Did Not Exceed 1989 PPP

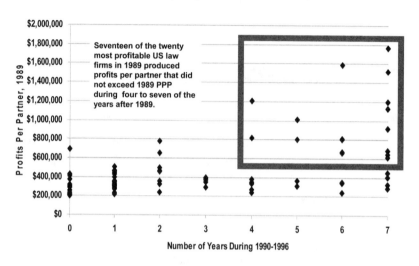

Number of Years During 1990-1996

This chart illustrates that, overall, the most profitable law firms suffer the longest recession impacts. For example, twelve Am Law 100 firms failed to produce higher PPP for *all seven* of the years following 1989; these firms included Cahill, Cravath, Davis Polk, Gibson Dunn, Kaye Scholer, O'Melveny, Paul Weiss, and Skadden. Eight more Am Law firms failed to exceed 1989 PPP for *six* of the following seven years; these firms included Kirkland, Latham, Milbank, Wachtell, and Willkie Farr.

Lower-end firms tolerate recessions better and recover from them faster.

The chart above also illustrates that those firms that generally feel a deep recession's impacts for the shortest time are less profitable firms with low billing rates and the lowest profits per partner. Even in depressed times, day-to-day legal work does not subside.

In this recession, many law firms will be dissolved or acquired by stronger firms.

I maintain a list of "weakest link" law firms—those that are nearing or have passed a tipping point in terms of falling lawyer headcount and net operating income (these two metrics seem to be better indicators of law firm dissolution and fire-sale acquisition than more arcane metrics). As of this writing, my "weakest links list" contains the names of nearly a dozen US law firms among the Am Law 200, the dissolution or acquisition of which would improve the health of competing firms, in some cases dramatically.

As with earlier recessions, this one will drive some law firms to failure and weaken other firms that will then fail after the recession ends. US regional markets that are particularly stressed include Atlanta, Boston, Ohio, and the San Francisco Bay Area. During this recession, we can also expect to see failures or acquisitions of three or four New York Am Law 100 and 200 firms.

Firms that grew *rapidly* in recent years, spending or borrowing heavily to fund their growth, will suffer extra pressures during this recession. Those pressures will be harder to withstand at firms where partners have been together only a short while.

These forecasts should not shock anyone. Of the Am Law 100 firms listed in reports describing 1989's financial performances, twenty no longer exist. Eight were acquired, and twelve have dissolved (see Table 2).

Table 2:   **Twenty 1989 Am Law 100 Firms That No Longer Exist**

Acquired by Other Firms	Dissolved
1. Brown & Wood	1. Arter & Hadden
2. Hale and Dorr	2. Brobeck, Phleger & Harrison
3. Hopkins & Sutter	3. Coudert Brothers
4. McCutchen, Doyle, Brown & Enersen	4. Gaston & Snow
5. Rogers & Wells	5. Graham & James
6. Rosenman & Colin	6. Heller Ehrman White & McAuliffe
7. Shaw Pittman	7. Johnson & Swanson
8. Winthrop, Stimson, Putnam & Roberts	8. Keck, Mahin & Cate
	9. Mudge Rose Guthrie Alexander & Ferdon
	10. Pettit & Martin
	11. Shea & Gould
	12. Thelen, Marrin, Johnson & Bridges

Stronger firms absorb failing firms' best assets, producing even stronger firms.

As in the past, many lawyers in firms that will fail or falter in the next few years will remain in private practice. An acquired firm's strongest assets (lawyers) with the best strategic fit will be retained and assimilated, or they will find even stronger new homes.

Newly acquired and unhappy groups and practices at unsteady firms will be fair game for poaching firms with the resources to invest in new talent.

Odds are also strong that another Magic Circle firm and a top-tier New York City firm will soon find more reasons to merge than to stay single. If I had more courage, I would name here those two firms I fantasize will tie the knot.

Many firms will return to a single equity partnership tier.

In the nineties, law firms created non-equity partnership tiers as a tactic to elevate their profits-per-partner performances. The number of non-equity partners grew in the 2000s, those ranks filled by reliable technicians who did good work and supplemented labor gaps unmet by the associate talent wars.

As a result, many firms now have expensive, middle-aged legal work forces with little appetite or aptitude to become equity partners. These non-equity partners supervise associates, a useful function, but one that has an unintended consequence of blocking mentoring of associates by equity partners. Traditionally, partner mentoring provided advice and development that helps talented, committed associates advance toward equity partnership themselves. Law firm associates' widespread and vocal dissatisfaction with their professional lot in the practice of law coincides with their insulation from partner mentoring.

Although few firms have yet announced they will eliminate completely their multiple partnership tiers, I often hear firm leaders talk about their desires to return to a single equity partnership structure. Therefore, I view some of the late 2008 and early 2009 partner downsizings as not only housecleaning and paring of practices, but efforts to reduce non-equity partnership tiers.

Legal marketing and business development functions will continue to evolve.

During the recession of 1990-91 and through the nineties, law firms began to engage marketers and marketing methods from other industries. This first wave of professional legal marketers focused on basic marketing services—promotional events, marketing communications, public relations, and branding. Marketing services have expanded over the years to include sales and sales support, decentralized marketing support for practice and industry groups, market research, in-house client feedback programs, and key client programs.

I predict that in the current downturn law firm marketing will undergo another renaissance. Marketing contributions that were valued 15-20 years ago probably will not make a big difference this time around.

Going forward, competitive firms will double down with even more professional sales support and coaching, key account management, and more sophisticated competitive intelligence functions. These skill sets will help firms to acquire, expand, and defend their best client relationships. In this global recession, law firms need the early-mover and better execution advantages these functions offer. These functions will also help firms add some badly needed rigor to their business planning function. Strategy, long pooh-poohed by most firm leaders, is finally seen to be important at both practice group and firm-wide levels.

Recessions Offer a Chance to Step Forward

Recessions offer opportunities for a law firm to emerge stronger than its competitors. Certainly, a law firm is obliged to do whatever it must to survive in the short term. But an equally important challenge for law firm leaders and their advisors is to find and take those positions (invest in resources) that will take advantage of changes wrought by the recession and the eventual recovery. Firms that will be stronger after this recession are those that find and tap new opportunities at the intersection of otherwise disconnected areas of expertise, where change is happening that they can exploit.

The changes offering opportunities to law firms in this recession are nearly limitless—energy and environmental changes, client industry changes, political changes, legislative and regulatory changes, as well as changes in the legal talent pool, law firm structures, fee arrangements, business processes, and legal technology.

The lessons of the 1990-91 recession tell us that fifteen years from now, a fifth of the today's "leading law firms" will no longer be around, having dissolved or been acquired by stronger firms. Others will have fallen one or more quartiles in the rankings that matter most—firm revenue, revenue per lawyer, and profits per equity partner. But still others will have ascended dramatically, having done what firms like Latham, Orrick, Dechert, Goodwin Procter, and Quinn Emanuel did in the last fifteen years—finding and tapping new opportunities at the intersection of otherwise disconnected areas of expertise, where change is happening that they can exploit. ●

22.
Re-thinking Your Global Strategy:
Geography, Talent and Management

Bruce MacEwen
Founder
"Adam Smith, Esq.," New York

*T*o give a composite of Bruce MacEwen's views on global growth for law firms, E. Leigh Dance wove this article together from excerpts of a number of recent posts on Bruce's famous blog, www.adamsmithesq. com. Bruce then edited it and gave his okay. The dates of the initial posts are provided, in case you want to refer back to the entire piece.

Globalization is surely one of the biggest buzzwords of our age. It means everything and nothing. As in the corporate sector, there's a perennial debate on how to manage global growth in a law firm. No matter how familiar the business issues for globalization might seem, it pays to revisit them. In good times, an unclear vision and suboptimal management can be overlooked; but at times like this there is no room for slack in the rigging.

129

Now is an ideal moment to re-examine the key assumptions in your global strategy (in fact, you should re-examine all the firm's key assumptions, but that's not my task here). Why now? Because lawyers' appetite for change, while never great, is at a maximum in the midst of disarray and uncertainty.

When clients and fees are rolling in, there's no sense of urgency about actually changing anything and, *a fortiori*, no reason to re-examine whether anything might be suboptimal. Today, everyone is tempted to ask, "What's wrong?!" It's a time when you can engage lawyers in actually taking steps to position your firm more soundly, for big payoff when things get better.

Global growth is not to be taken lightly, and critical thinking is required in at least three areas: geography, talent, and what I'll call management structure and leadership. This essay is a combination of posts in the last year on those three topics.

One caveat before we jump in: focus your critical thinking out to the horizon. Try to get a sighting of Muscat or Hangzhou in your binoculars. Flip your calendar to 2014. Managing a law firm is not an exercise in quarter to quarter or year to year performance. Just as the transition of a market from 'emerging' to 'emerged' will take decades, the transition from national firm to truly global firm will take much more time than you wish.

Where You Go (*from posts of 4 April 08 and 22 Aug. 08*)

In their financial data released in August 2008, Citicorp pointed out that "international" firms, (defined as those with 10 to 25% of their lawyers abroad) "experienced greater profit margin compression than any other group of firms." By contrast, "global" firms, with more than 25% of their lawyers abroad, experienced the least profit margin compression. All that may have changed, but the contrast is indeed instructive when looking at a long time horizon.

If you assume that firms just beginning, or in the early stages, of international expansion are focused on the UK and the EU, this makes some sense—expansion in those markets is very costly. Moreover, besides the US, those geographies are hurting the most from the economic crisis. By contrast, assuming Citi's definition of "global" firm identifies firms farther down the globalization path, they're likely to have substantial presences in a broader range of emerging markets in Asia and the Middle East. Those markets are suffering relatively less.

Most importantly, this speaks to the power of a diversified portfolio of practices—both by specialty and by geography. Globalization is here to stay, and the notion of a powerhouse firm based primarily in one country—no matter how large the domestic economy—will increasingly become a mark of irrelevance.

So, what's to be done? You can begin by looking fresh at the familiar landscape:
- geographic or product area focus?
- heavily centralized or with greater local customization?
- capitalizing on cross-border synergies or maximizing local, country-specific practices?

The fundamental challenge is to capture the greatest value from local practices while also benefiting from the value of an international platform and brand.

What sense does the geographic array of your offices make? Ought you to be in (just to pick a random place) London in a bigger way than you are? Does Frankfurt/Miami/Seattle (pick one or three) still make sense? What about the emerging/emerged markets (see below)?

If you could re-draw you firm's global breadth and depth on a clean sheet of paper and then connect the dots, what would it look like?

Eye on Emerging Markets *(from a 1 Sept. 08 post)*

The world is vastly different from August 2008 when McKinsey presented the emerging markets opportunities highlighted in its Global Capital Markets Survey (article by Markus Bohme, Daniele Chiarella and Matthieu Lemerle). McKinsey projected that revenues from investment-banking and capital market activities in the emerging markets of Asia, Europe, the Middle East and Latin America would match those in North America by 2010. In 2006, before the credit crunch, they amounted to less than half.

Why are these markets so attractive? For one thing, they're already getting sophisticated. A new breed of global corporate players, notably in countries such as China, India, and the United Arab Emirates (UAE), now demands *the sort of sophisticated services [and concomitant legal services] previously reserved for large Western multinationals.* This new group thus represents an increasingly attractive fee pool.

Other reinforcing trends are in play. Certainly in Asia, economies are still growing on their own. As Asia becomes increasingly integrated with the global economy, inbound and outbound investment will grow, and it will take increasingly sophisticated forms. For "sophistication," substitute "lawyer-heavy," and you have a reason to take this region more seriously.

Do you have to be there? I believe you do. But let McKinsey speak to this:

Asian markets are fast becoming as demanding and sophisticated as markets in Europe and the United States. Clients are operating in the same complex regulatory and financial landscape as their western counterparts, and have developed a taste for sophisticated, integrated advice and good local service. Domestic competitors are ramping up their skills and vying for international talent. An onshore presence is becoming critical—you need to be *in* the local market.

And the Middle East? Corporations are deploying more management professionals to the region, as it becomes a hub for an emerging world that includes Africa. The states of the Gulf Cooperation Council (GCC)—Bahrain, Kuwait, Oman, Qatar, Saudi Arabia, and the UAE—have been generating wealth at levels not seen since the 1980s. While lower oil prices have slowed the wave of investment, there are numerous industrial and large-scale infrastructure projects in progress. Can you afford to miss this? That is for your firm to call, including your partners' appetite for risk and their willingness to endure a period of potentially protracted investment. But the historic shift of momentum seems clear: emerging markets offer a rare window of opportunity.

Stack your Odds for Success *(from a 12 May 08 post)*

Global expansion is scary. Most firms have been burned once or twice, and many lawyers today will be skittish about adding more risks to their daily worries. They have a point. According to a McKinsey study* in the corporate world, <u>four out of every five</u> attempts to enter a new market fails. This isn't limited to startups or novice businesses; it includes very sophisticated firms. (* "Beating the odds in market entry: how to avoid cognitive biases that undermine market entry decisions," by John T. Horn, Dan P. Lovallo and S. Patrick Viguerie, Nov. 2005)

So how can you re-think your strategy to improve your odds? According to McKinsey, there are three elements which need to work in your favor to launch into a new market successfully:

> • Timing. Never underestimate this. How many firms went piling into Silicon Valley shortly before the dot-com bust? And how many are opening in Dubai, Abu Dhabi, and Qatar with the "sovereign wealth" mantra? Not all will come to tears, by any means, but it's worth asking searching questions about the durability of those trends.

> • Scale relative to the competition: Can you viably enter with anything resembling critical mass and, if not, how long will it take to get it, and what it will cost in the interim? Law firms are famously allergic to long-term investments, because they have to be funded out of current (after-tax) income. But if you're not serious about invading certain markets, best not try.

> • Whether the new market complements your existing strengths. It might make sense for Texas-based energy firms to launch in Kazakhstan, but why do so many commercial firms think that they need to be dragon slayers in London?

Since these preconditions for success are so obvious, why do we see such a high failure rate? McKinsey believes executives make "systematic errors in processing information" such as:

> • Believing the potential market is bigger than it is;

> • Failing to consider the certitude that rivals will respond; and/or

> • Relying heavily on "inside" views and opinions rather than trying to develop an untainted, outside perspective premised on the track record of similar attempted market penetrations.

To address the last point, you should assemble some examples of similar attempted market penetrations by other firms in the past. Once you have your precedents assembled, bring in a "Red Team" to play the role of devil's advocate, seeking out flaws in your analysis, anticipating potential competitive responses, coldly gauging the investment required and the time frame, and, in general, seeking to avoid the myopic but all too human tendency to seek out confirming data and ignore or discount contradictory information or analyses. (The term "Red Team" comes from CIA parlance, standing for the team designed to attack the strategy of the good guys, the "Blue Team.")

Global Warfare: Talent *(from a 16 May 08 post)*
The next part of the global strategy re-think is to take a hard look at your people and how you manage them. Do these descriptions fit your firm, or sound credible to you?

> • "Managing our talent globally is far more complex and demanding than it is domestically."

> • "The movement of employees between countries is still surprisingly limited."

> • "Many people tempted to relocate internationally fear that doing so will damage their career prospects."

Welcome to the international 'war for talent.' As McKinsey reported in spring 2008,** companies that can satisfy their global talent needs and overcome cultural and other silo-based barriers tend to outperform those that don't. (** "Why multinationals struggle to manage talent," Matthew Guthridge and Asmus B. Komm, May 08)

McKinsey's study involved in-depth interviews with executives at 11 major global corporations and includes responses of senior managers at 22 other global companies (more than 450 people in all), about how their firms deal with the challenge of talent management.

To be specific, if financial performance is measured by profit per employee, there is a very high correlation between companies that score in the top third of the survey on ten dimensions of global talent management, and profitability. In particular, companies scoring in the top third on any one of three critical dimensions of talent management stood a 70% chance of achieving top-third financial performance. The top three most important practices are: (a) "ensuring global consistency in management processes;" (b) "achieving cultural diversity in global setting;" and (c) "developing and managing global leaders."

Why is consistency in talent evaluation across all geographic regions so important? Simply because if mobility is to be a reality, managers need confidence that people transferring into (or back to) their practice areas have met the same standards.

Companies that consistently differentiated themselves from their competitors excelled at:

•Top management encouraging people to get experience across multiple locations;

• Regarding overseas experience as essentially a prerequisite for promotion to senior-most levels; and

• Offering managers incentives to "lose" their most talented employees to other functions or geographies.

The cocoon of your departmental, practice group, and geographic "silo" is no position from which to become truly global. Devote serious senior management time to exploding those comfortable silos, and encouraging (and rewarding) global mobility and coordination. Otherwise the unspoken but irrepressible suspicion of the foreign will derail your fondest hopes of achieving the "one-firm firm."

Management Structure and Leadership (from a July 2nd post)
In an enlightening interview in *Knowledge@Wharton* (http://knowledge. wharton.upenn.edu) with William Weldon, CEO of Johnson & Johnson, we can learn a lot about the leadership and management structure needed for a global law firm. You may think the scale of J&J (120,000 employees, $61-billion in revenue, operations in multiple dozens of countries) means

there's no analog between what he does and what you do. Think again. In addition to deciding where you go and who will produce your revenues, what is the overarching new challenge for a multi-office international law firm? It's leadership and management of a fundamentally decentralized organization.

As a law firm, your offices, practice groups, and even individual client teams operate with a very high level of autonomy, certainly by the standards of corporate America. Weldon describes that with over 200 operating companies at J&J, even if he devoted a full day to each operating company, it would take him the entire year to cycle through all of them. He accepts that they will operate mostly autonomously. Is, then, running such an enormous organization fundamentally impossible or impracticable? Not at all; he sees advantages to it.

Weldon says, "I think J&J is probably the reference company for being decentralized. There are challenges to it, and that is you may not have as much control as you may have in a centralized company.

"If you look at Japan, for example, we have the local management running the companies. They understand the consumer, they understand the people they are dealing with and they understand the government and the needs in the marketplace. Whereas it's very hard to run it from the US and to think that we would know enough to be able to do this. [...] But, with our credo and the value system that we work under, we feel very confident about our leadership and our management [...] "I think the other thing that decentralization does is that it gives you a tremendous opportunity to develop people. You give them a lot of opportunity to work in different areas, to work in smaller companies, to make mistakes and to ultimately move to larger companies."

There's much in here:

• You sacrifice control but you gain great people, who develop into leaders, assuming you have "a lot of confidence and faith in them."

• You get your operations closer to the ground, closer to the customer, and for that matter closer to the regulatory authorities.

• But—and this may be challenge #1 for law firm leaders—you have to be realistic about ceding control and realistic about people "making mistakes."

Perhaps the supreme and ongoing challenge for J&J is maintaining the pace of innovation. With the huge changes in global legal services demand, this is important for law firms. How does Weldon describe how J&J pursues innovation?

It starts with decentralization, another important lesson for globally growing law firms. "Where decentralization helps in innovation is that it allows different people with different skills, different thoughts, to bring together different products and technologies to satisfy the unmet needs of patients or customers."

Weldon says (emphasis supplied): "*It's the ability to work across the boundaries that really brings true innovation*, and is going to take some real breakthroughs and will bring real breakthroughs in the future. But, it also does take some coordination and some sacrifice from the individual. *That is the toughest thing, getting people to get outside of the silos that they work in* and work across the groups."

"By being decentralized; what you do lose is control. But, with our credo and the value system that we work under, we feel very confident about our leadership and our management."

The key phrase is "with our credo and value system." Is that something you can say with equal confidence about your firm? Do your partners, associates, and staff *around the world* live your firm's values? Because if they don't, decentralization is not a viable option for your firm. Even more strongly, don't even think about successful global expansion. Without a unified worldwide credo, you'd be delusional even to try. ●

23.
LAW FIRM 4.0
Considerations for the Global Law Firm in 2020

Deborah McMurray
CEO and Strategy Architect
Content Pilot LLC, Dallas

We're at a unique time in history. Global financial analysts are calling what happened in the equity markets in 2008 "unprecedented." The "2009 Outlook Ahead—U.S. Sector Strategy" by Merrill Lynch (the financial services giant acquired by Bank of America in September 2008) is guarded, but overall, the view is optimistic.

Merrill Lynch identified "three primary investment themes for US equities for 2009:

1. Slowing global growth, and the resulting impact of a stronger US dollar.

2. Balance sheet strength of corporate America – especially in terms of high cash levels, steady cash flow and decreased leverage.

3. Increased conservatism–moderation of corporate and consumer spending."

These three themes set the stage for this discussion of "Law Firm 4.0." They will affect clients of law firms for years to come, and will therefore affect regional, national and global law firm choices.

Rethink and Re-imagine the Law Firm Business Model

If you were starting your law firm today, what would you do differently? Most of today's law firm leaders inherited clients, infrastructure, locations, practices, policies and governance structure, and more from the firm's previous generations of lawyer leaders. Culture and inertia are powerful forces in law firms, and even de minimis change is resisted by firm stalwarts, from secretaries to partners. So, the most forward-thinking, concerned law firm leaders run into obstacles that make sweeping, top-to-bottom change almost impossible.

Already in this new century, we've seen an industry boom quickly dissolve to bust. Wall Street investment banks, Fortune 500 companies and their law firms report record profits, and in 2008, we saw the best brand names in home-building and construction experience revenue decline by 80% or more, the US automotive industry essentially fail and financial services and the storied Wall Street firms go bankrupt or end up in a fire sale. We've also witnessed prestigious, old law firms who were so closely tied to these industries fail or struggle to survive with double-digit percentage decreases in lawyers and staff, and much lower revenue and profit.

There is an opportunity for today's leaders who have the right attributes—vision, courage, accountability, blocking and tackling skills—to rethink the business model for tomorrow's law firm. There will be another boom and most assuredly, another bust. The lawyers who understand the lessons in today's turbulence and don't repeat the folly and sins of the past have the best chance to shape the future that they want.

The December 2008 issue of *Harvard Business Review* features an article called, "Reinventing your Business Model" by Mark W. Johnson, Clayton M. Christensen and Henning Kagermann. Two statements struck me: *"One secret to maintaining a thriving business is recognizing when it needs a fundamental change,"* and *"Business model innovations have reshaped entire industries and redistributed billions of dollars of value."*

The authors state that, while everyone's talking about business model innovation, there have been "precious few" innovations in global companies over the last decade that were business model related. They note that a 2008 IBM survey of corporate CEOs reported the need to adapt their business models, and more than two-thirds said "extensive changes are required." Many are looking at business model innovation "to address permanent shifts in their market landscapes." So, if our clients are doing it both to survive and thrive, law firms should be doing it, too.

The First Step: Identify What's Getting in your Way

The HBR article includes a handy list for companies, broken out into financial, operational and other things to analyze and consider as you rethink your business model. They warn that rules, norms and metrics protect your status quo and can thwart progress. I have taken the HBR list and redefined them below for law firms.

FINANCIAL	OPERATIONAL	OTHER
Gross revenue/profits per partner/profits per equity partner/revenue per lawyer	Quality of legal services	Target industries and geographic markets
Growth or decline from existing clients	Quality of suppliers, vendors, consultants	Practice mix and practice life-cycles
Opportunity size from new clients and opportunity cost	Outsourcing: legal processes (LPO) and business processes (BPO)	Pricing of services
Associate salaries and cost of recruiting	Client relationship management/client service	Service and delivery innovation

FINANCIAL	OPERATIONAL	OTHER
Fixed cost investments	Strength/sophistication of professional and administrative departments	Brand value, enhancement and growth
Credit availability and cost	Lawyer to staff ratios	Business development
Malpractice and other insurance	Facilities maintenance and management	
Bonuses, rewards and incentives	Essential support services for lawyers	

Adapted for law firms from the article by Johnson, Christensen, Kagermann, *Harvard Business Review*, Dec. 2008

These lists aren't exhaustive, but they are a good start. Understand where old thinking preserves old behaviors, and push to zero-base your thinking in each of these key areas.

Law Firm 4.0: Considerations for Change
The following common functions or departments in law firms require examination because they meet one or more of these criteria:
1. They are ripe for change
2. They are forgotten or overlooked
3. The mere cost of them in the annual budget makes them a target
4. They make clients angry.

Legal Service Delivery: Staffing and Ultimately, Recruiting
The Association of Corporate Counsel (ACC) launched The ACC Value Challenge in 2008, a program it says "reconnects cost with value." Leaders of ACC have spoken at numerous legal industry conferences about this initiative, and the General Counsel, Susan Hackett, had an interview in the December 2008 *American Lawyer,* called "Peace Talks." The Value Challenge presentation focuses heavily on staffing of matters and how corporate legal departments are refusing (or will refuse) to pay

for inexperienced associates on their matters. This griping has been going on for years, but little has been done to bridge the value gap.

Hackett notes that Howrey is one firm that has stepped out; it is not charging for first-year associates' time on client matters. She reports the early result of this: legal departments are now happy to have these young lawyers as team members, and happy to mentor them and guide them on both lawyer/client relationship issues and the specifics of the legal matter. They are getting solid training and experience, but the firm is footing that bill, not the client. Below are four other ideas to consider.

Idea 1: New internship approach. Could we design a law firm internship program similar to what medical schools and teaching hospitals have done? This would require much lower first and second year salaries for associates and commitment by these interns to work hard, but there would be a guarantee of the best work and training. Salaries would bump up considerably in years three and four, so perhaps associates would see enough of a carrot to stay at the firms longer. According to the ACC presentation, law firms spend on average $450,000 per first year associate before their first day of employment. With first year compensation at or around $200,000 and typical attrition, large law firms have little hope of ever breaking even with today's recruiting model.

Idea 2: "Teaching" law firms. Perhaps the medical profession could be the harbinger of what's to come in another respect: Certain hospitals are teaching hospitals, and many others are not. Interns at teaching hospitals build their careers outside their original hospitals—in private practice, as members of clinics, as physicians in other hospitals. Why couldn't a few top law firms be the designated training ground for the best law graduates in the country? They become the teaching hospital equivalent. Then, when the associates become "residents," they would interview and find the jobs around the world that best fit their skills and dreams.

Hundreds of US law firms collectively invest millions each year in summer programs and associate recruiting. All this duplication of effort to recruit the same top 10% with predictably similar results year after year, firm to firm—well, it's crying out for rethinking at a minimum, and better, a Law Firm 4.0 business model.

Idea 3: Placement of associate hires. Only hire associates in your city locations with the lowest cost of living. Staff your most important client matters with senior partners (wherever the best ones live), but only use lower cost associates who live elsewhere. This can significantly reduce the cost of service delivery, because salaries and their hourly rates are lower, and you don't have to lease the most expensive office space in the world to house them. Several global law firms are already doing this, but they aren't quite ready to publicize it.

Idea 4: "Engagement Partners" for Major Clients. This next idea has nothing to do with recruiting or young lawyers. It is about ensuring that every institutional (or important) client has the best client service lawyer and technical partner on the job. For decades, the major accounting firms have appointed engagement partners for key clients. While many global law firm partners serve as "key client relationship partners," there are elements of the Big 4 approach described below that law firms could adopt to further raise the superior service delivery bar.

Big 4 leaders conduct a national search within their ranks to identify the best technical partners, who are chosen because of their proven performance in the client's industry and with the client's type of company. Because key clients are truly institutional, these partners may or may not have had any previous service responsibility to the client. The engagement partner manages the work and the team, and the Fortune 100 company clients also have a client service partner, who assures continuous, extraordinary service and focuses not on the technical aspects, but on the relationship.

Because the engagement partners have a mandatory rotation out after five years for public companies, there is virtually no danger of lateral defection with the plum client in tow. The terms of the client service partners don't expire. If in-house legal departments work harder to adopt the "hire the law firm, not the lawyer" shift proposed by ACC, then law firms must follow with a responsive business model, perhaps closer to the Big 4. Global, multi-office law firms are particularly suited to this new staffing and relationship structure.

Marketing and Business Development

Since the birth of this industry in the 1980s, law firms have made higher demands and marketing professionals have responded. Looking out a decade or more, there is great opportunity to re-imagine the marketing department, its functions and structure, not necessarily to reduce cost, but to raise its contribution to top line revenue and bottom line profit.

Idea 1: Separate marketing operations from business growth. The buck has to stop somewhere, and I still support a Chief Marketing Officer as the leader and overseer of these functions. But the department model where marketers serve everyone in the law firm, regardless of the request, is no longer viable. There are three primary reasons: 1) This approach can't support a strategic plan. Pet initiatives are invented by individuals, not designed to meet strategic firm or practice goals. In this old but familiar model, marketers must serve firm leaders, rainmakers and less productive lawyers equally. In many cases, they are criticized for serving the masses, yet also admonished by the under-served for not serving everyone. 2) Lawyers get inconsistent access, service, advice and expertise from a department of even the most willing generalists. And 3) marketers suffer burnout faster, and finding and retaining terrific marketers is as difficult as it is with lawyers.

Instead, organize responsibilities into two major functional areas—marketing operations and business growth. "Operations" would include your integrated marketing infrastructure that supports sales and business development—for example, marketing databases, technologies, Web site, marketing finance, tracking and measurement, PR, graphic design, advertising, collateral development, event planning and various concierge services.

The appropriate marketing and business development mix should vary from practice to practice. Consider the vastly different marketing resources one should employ to support certain mature practices or relationships versus growing and expanding new practices, industries and markets. Successful global growth initiatives require great investment of time, planning, energy and money. Programs that are less far reaching will require less.

The other functional area is "business growth." The business development team should help lawyers analyze the best opportunities for business growth in the firm, and be involved in designing the client team around the client needs rather than being driven by the legacy lawyer relationships. This has its own infrastructure and resource requirements described in *"Idea 2"* below. Increasingly, business development professionals are sought after by major law firms, but in most cases, they are forced to work within a non-innovative business model. Consequently, the attrition rate is high, often at a high cost to the firm. Until a rigorous sales process is adopted and proven by a pilot group or two, and until the firm embraces this proven process going forward—because it works—law firm business development will continue to be centered only around those who like it and have the courage and discipline to pursue it.

In many firms regardless of size or reach, the ratio of rainmakers is low, estimated by firm leaders at 8-12% of all lawyers in the firm. For firms to markedly enhance revenue and profit, the number of producers must increase.

Idea 2: Build the necessary infrastructure. To support business growth initiatives, lawyers and the business development group need the right infrastructure. This includes competitive intelligence (not just competitive information), scenario planning and financial analysis, client loyalty and feedback programs, sales and other training, and technology and systems that are Web-based and multi-purpose—tracking accountability, leveraging knowledge across borders, including fingertip retrieval of deals, cases and matters, collaborating across offices and time zones, logging and connecting opportunities in multiple offices and noting where they are in the pipeline, and more. All this frees up human capital so the team can focus on strategic ways to win business, not the tactical elements, such as proposal assembly and document management.

Then, after *every* major pitch or proposal, conduct formal win/ loss interviews and analyses. Learn why you won or lost and make the appropriate changes in your approach to this and future clients. The key to driving more business from these interviews (or any client interview) is the disciplined follow up—tracking the effectiveness and result of changes the next time. This is one of the surest relationship enhancement vehicles available to firms today, yet few firms build the cost of these interviews into their budgets. Make both planning and debriefing equally disciplined.

Conclusion

At the start of *"Seize Advantage in a Downturn,"* a February 2009 article in *Harvard Business Review* authors David Rhodes and Daniel Stelter (both global partners with Boston Consulting Group, from London and Berlin respectively), state, "A downturn opens up rare opportunities to outmaneuver rivals. But first you need to put your own house in order." Minimize vulnerabilities today and set the stage for planned and aggressive rival out-maneuvering.

Many global law firms manage their budgets well, and have trimmed excesses so that overhead cost is streamlined and efficient. Firms who are seeking ways to cut further, often target marketing and business development. Authors Rhodes and Stelter state, "Companies that injudiciously slash marketing spending often find that they later must spend far more than they saved in order to recover."

Resist the temptation to take the easier route of wholesale budget slashing. Rather, take a 30,000-foot view of your business model and get closer to Law Firm 4.0 strategies. The innovations that result will not only help you manage your top and bottom line better today and in the future, it will ensure you a leader-of-the-pack position among your rivals. ●

24.
How Corporate Counsel in the UK and Europe are Changing, and the Key Elements of Success

Mary Mullally
Practical Law Company, London

Ten years of boom times have been good to in-house counsel in the UK and Europe; their status has never been better. But the proof of the pudding will be how they fare in poor economic conditions and crucially whether they can deliver real value when the going gets tough.

In 1999 when I was working as a junior legal reporter I covered a story about a leading building society axing of 20 of a 32 strong legal department. A spokesperson told me that the business had made the decision to cut the in-house team because "it was just as effective to buy the best in the market." He added, "I suspect that other companies are quietly making similar cuts."

His prediction was ill founded. The last decade has seen a huge growth in the size of legal functions in businesses across the UK and Europe and this growth, until very recently, looked set to continue.

In a PLC Law Department Benchmarking Survey* in June 2008,

admittedly before the credit crunch crisis truly hit, over half of the senior in-house lawyers questioned said that they had increased the size of their team in the last year and planned to make increases in the next year, with only 2% indicating that they planned cuts.

At the same time it was clear that law departments were planning to bring more work in-house, with a massive 73% of those questioned indicating that the current economic climate had led them to internalise more legal work rather than outsource it to law firms.

These findings are indicative of a huge surge in confidence among in-house counsel over this side of the pond. In the early 90s it was not so unusual for in-house counsel to be viewed as second rate by their private practice counterparts and as a back office function by the businesses they served. This has all changed. And it is those who head up the departments who have led the way.

In the US, General Counsel have long been perceived as the trusted adviser with close access to the board. Ten years ago this was rarely the case in the UK and Europe. But the senior in-house lawyer of ten years ago is a very different animal from today.

This has been driven to a certain extent by globalization; most of the companies that now operate in the UK are multinational players and are looking for a new breed of in-house lawyer greatly influenced by the US model. There are a number of key trends that reflect this:

• All but a handful of the largest companies now have a "general counsel" or equivalent. General Counsel increasingly sit within the heart of the businesses that they advise and have the "ear of the board" where it matters. In another survey * this year over three quarters of general counsel attended board meetings as an observer or adviser particularly in relation to risk and governance issues.

• The range of responsibilities that sit within the general counsel fold has grown. It is increasingly typical to see a general counsel advising the board on areas that would not have fallen within their remit ten years ago; responsibilities typically can include: corporate governance; human resources; risk and compliance;

corporate social responsibility; share schemes; and insurance and pensions.

• Increasingly general counsel report in to the CEO. 60% of general counsel this year indicated that they report directly to the CEO of the company, compared to around 50% in 2005 and 36% in 2003.

• There is also a marked trend for general counsel to take on non-executive positions either in tandem with their role of general counsel or on retirement.

It is worth pointing out there is still a gap between those in-house counsel operating in the UK and their European counterparts. The proportion of general counsel that report into the CEO is lower on the continent. Their profile and status within the companies which they serve often lags behind their UK counterparts. There are however signs that they are following the UK and US lead and all indications are that the US model is beginning to dominate irrespective of jurisdiction.

This new style of General Counsel needs a new skill set; a strong legal background is a given but a broader range of experience and expertise is now a prerequisite for the role. Commercial acumen; communication skills; and an ability to build relationships and strong management skills are the qualities that are likely to mark out the General Counsel of the next decade.

At this time more than ever business needs general counsel of this calibre to help them through unchartered legal territory.

But while it is important to be at the top table and have the ear of the board, against a background of unprecedented economic turmoil the ability to deliver on the bottom line and harness resources effectively is also likely to be a key factor in determining those who succeed and those who fail.

In the current economic climate in-house departments have no choice but to wake up to the need to drive efficiency. With more legal work and less resource they have two options – send out to the law firms at huge expense or look at alternative strategies to build efficiency into the way in which they do business.

The last decade has seen a round of complaints about spiralling law firm fees with little action on the part of in-house counsel to really address how they can drive efficiency both internally and through their legal advisers.

Signs are that this is beginning to change already, with many UK and European departments exploring initiatives such as off-shoring work to cheaper jurisdictions; legal process outsourcing; and the automation and standardisation of documents with a view to driving down the costs of the legal function.

Now that general counsel and their teams are firmly entrenched across the business, the real test has come; have they earned the right to remain there?

The decision does not lie with the legal department but with the business. The next year or so will provide a significant indication of how much companies in the UK and Europe really value their in-house advisers and how much value their in-house advisers really deliver....in the bad times as well as the good. ●

*PLC Law Department benchmarking series http://ld.practicallaw.com/7-205-4441

25.
The Key to Credible International Branding

Norm Rubenstein
Partner
Zeughauser Group, Washington DC

Virtually all law firm web sites trumpet unparalleled legal work, legendary service, a zealous commitment to cost-effectiveness, and access to creative, collaborative, and highly ethical lawyers. Moreover, they imply a caliber of legal product and a service experience vastly superior to that which other law firms can provide. Since those claims are mirrored by those of their competitors, it is no wonder that clients and recruits are increasingly critical of a universe of seemingly fungible law firms.

If quality, service, and price traditionally have defined legal marketing's thematic trinity, a new claim has emerged in the last decade: the concept of the global law firm—that is, a firm that promises both sophistication and experience in supporting cross-border deals, interpreting the effects of local and international regulation, and resolving disputes in one or many of its myriad locations.

Perhaps no claim is more frequently cited these days than a law firm's "international" cred, and none has been less convincingly substantiated. Let's look, for a moment, at the process by which in-house counsel or business professionals with the authority to hire outside counsel identify potential law firms or lawyers. Most start with the referral process—that is, they seek advice from respected colleagues. In situations where they need more information or want to vet or supplement what they have learned, they likely peruse law firms' web sites or consult one of the few rating services or directories whose methodologies they trust (e.g., Chambers).

Armed with a sense of which firms might provide the right combination of expertise, experience, and value, legal service buyers next must select among a smaller list of firms making similar claims. And this is where clients increasingly argue that law firm web sites, advertising, and other external communication materials not only fail to differentiate among service providers, but also suggest a significant and systemic disconnect between what they want and what firms trumpet.

Authentic and Aspirational

Realistically, an effective law firm brand must be simultaneously authentic and aspirational. It must convey the firm's practice, footprint, and culture in ways that are verifiable by clients, prospects, recruits, and the media, among other interested audiences. As importantly, it must feel authentic to firm members and employees. Practically, in an age of unrelenting consolidation, legal brands must evidence sufficient elasticity to allow for firm growth and a perpetually evolving strategy. Indeed, narrow brand platforms that must be rearticulated following every significant growth event inevitably create confusion in the legal marketplace.

However, a quick perusal of the Global 50 or of the AmLaw 100 reveals a cadre of large, multi-practice firms with footprints that stretch around the globe and principal brand messaging emphasizing their international status. Firms like to define their reach by their clients' markets, which means that virtually every law firm in our evolving economy can make a legitimate claim to being international. But it is one thing to say that one advises businesses with expanding international interests and another altogether to suggest that a global practice is a firm's hallmark or trump suit.

In a globalizing economy, it is no surprise that law firms strive to be seen as international. As an increasing number of deals, disputes, and regulatory challenges cross borders, beleaguered in-house legal departments are forced to manage dispersed legal activities with inadequate resources and, as a response, they turn to outside counsel for both specialized expertise and global reach. But the important question that law firms must address (and I would posit to date have not addressed effectively) is whether they appreciate what clients understand the promise—the value proposition—of an international law firm actually should be.

Overemphasis on Size and Scope

Study electronic and printed law firm marketing from large multinational law firms and "international" often equates to the display of an impressive physical plant and expanding lawyer workforce. Indeed, a casual perusal of large "international" law firm web sites reveals thousands of lawyers and a footprint with dozens of offices on multiple continents. In other words, the proof points for claiming to be "international" relate primarily to size and scope.

I would submit that when clients and prospects (and, indeed, even recruits) survey the brands of self-designated international law firms, they conclude that law firms mean something entirely different than they do about what it means to be an effective global law firm. A better answer— and one more closely aligned with client concerns—well might focus on the execution of a philosophical commitment to collaboration.

When a client hires outside counsel to assist it with a matter in another jurisdiction (read for jurisdiction: city, state, or country), it is looking for a firm that appreciates the nuances of bringing together a team of highly experienced local practitioners and maximizing the contribution that they make individually and collectively. Whether the firm has an office and lawyers on the ground in one or more of the places where the client's work requires expertise and attention, or whether it commits to finding proxies for its own lawyers among members of a global network or among an affiliation of independently identified firms, the focus should not simply be on being everywhere, but on working strategically and compatibly with culturally diverse lawyers who understand and appreciate the clients' issues and concerns in its many geographies. That focus must relate both to substance and service delivery.

This shift in frame of reference away from numbers—whether it be numbers of offices or head count—to a manner of practicing requires law firms to accept that what clients want, what they are buying, is comfort with both the way that the firm practices and its promise that it will accept responsibility for orchestrating appropriate local counsel, expertise, and execution on the client's behalf. A significant part of that implied promise is not just that the firm will acquire capability it lacks—whether that is expertise at appropriate levels of sophistication greater than its own lawyers can provide or in areas where it has no extant practice—but that its *own* lawyers universally subscribe to consistent practice and service standards.

Demonstrating the Brand's Validity

Many clients have experienced unevenness in the quality of the work product or in the service delivery and communication standards of lawyers in their outside firms' other offices, and that experience has led to the widespread suspicion that large, multi-office, multi-practice firms more closely resemble franchises than integrated entities. What many clients believe they are acquiring when they pay the fees of a global law firm is the firm's lawyers' ability to address issues across geographies and, therefore, provide the client with a better response. So a law firm sensitive to that historical concern might distinguish itself by focusing its messaging on the way in which it both has sustained the experiential and substantive integrity and local focus of its lawyers in every market while inculcating a commitment to client service and satisfaction that transcends the idiosyncrasies of individual lawyers or cultures.

The trick to branding that confirms this message platform is demonstration, not claim. And in an age in which electronic communication better serves the needs of both sender and recipient, the medium well might be web sites or e-alerts as opposed to conventional brochures (although targeted advertising might be an effective tie-in with such a campaign.) A global law firm needs a section for case studies that illustrate its capacity to work across borders in ways that advantage its clients. Those brief descriptions of a problem solved or an opportunity realized for a client must describe not only the "what" of the matter, but the "how." Featuring a current one on the site's home page, with links to a compendium of other case studies featuring initiatives that underscore the firm's seamless communication and collaboration across borders would suggest that this is more than rhetoric—it is a legitimate spotlight on a key client priority that differentiates the firm from its competitors.

When law firms demonstrate an appreciation that global is about making the world accessible, manageable and even predictable, in the best of ways, their primary marketing messaging will supplant or enhance the precedent-sanctioned claims of quality, responsiveness, and value—and now of international focus. What will emerge will be a new focus on the integrity of the firm's vision and execution and how a demonstrable philosophy of practice can yield true benefits for clients as well as a platform of irresistible caliber for recruits. To market in a manner more compelling than that which we have seen to date from firms positioning themselves as international would be to tell real stories that demonstrate to clients and other audiences that the firm has achieved the grail of cross-border alignment—not simply to claim that the firm exists in Abu Dhabi, Tokyo, and Rio de Janeiro as well as in New York and London. ●

26.
A Foot in the Past, a Finger on the Pulse, and an Eye to the Future: What it Takes to be an Exceptional Global Law Firm Leader

Simon Slater
Director
First Counsel, London

1994. Bill Clinton was one year into his presidency. Nelson Mandela was elected South Africa's first black president. Tony Blair became leader of the Labour Party in the UK, and China had the seventh largest GDP in the world, just behind the UK.

Remember when we lived in a world without broadband and Blackberrys? A time when we conducted business without the aid of Google, pod-casts, blogs and Skype? When we communicated, shopped, travelled and relaxed without the aid of iPhones, Facebook, Wikipedia, Amazon, eBay, Sat Nav, iPods and Wiis? Fifteen years ago the World-Wide-Web was just two years old as far as Joe Public was concerned. The world was still driven by people and bricks rather than domain-names and clicks.

Organizations which had operations across the world's major territories were described as international rather than global. There *was* no globalization. The West was clearly the dominant economic force. And nobody talked about on-line and offline, or commoditization, outsourcing, co-sourcing and off-shoring.

In the legal industry in 1994, lawyers were supported by staff who were mostly secretaries and back-office administrators. There was only one substantial international law firm. There were certainly no law firm chairmen or chief executives; practice leaders were still senior and managing partners. There were a few early partnership secretaries, practice directors and heads of finance, but that's about it. There were virtually no LLPs or LLCs. Precious few law firms had web sites or intranets, and there were very few practice support lawyers (PSLs) or "knowledge managers." No-one talked about Generation X, let alone Y. Law firm panels had not yet taken root and all was calm and cosy in the world of the successful law firm.

Fifteen years ago, Baker & McKenzie was that law firm—the world's largest. By then, it had blazed a trail for a largely sceptical legal profession, building a practice with around 1,800 lawyers in 32 countries. The accountancy market was dominated by the "Big 6" (remember Arthur Andersen?), and Price Waterhouse and Coopers & Lybrand were separate firms.

How times appear to have changed.

The world's largest law firms are now Baker & McKenzie and Clifford Chance. Each has in excess of 3,800 lawyers and some 7,000 staff in total, and revenues of well over $2 billion. Baker & McKenzie now has 70 offices across the globe, whilst Clifford Chance has pursued a less expansive geographical footprint. Nonetheless, a small number of European firms now dominate the global legal services market alongside a similar number of their US-led counterparts.

And yet, legal practices are still relative minnows in comparison with other globalized organizations. PricewaterhouseCoopers (PwC), the world's largest professional services firm, is 10 times the size of Clifford Chance; Exxon Mobil, the world's largest corporation, is 200 times its size.

So how valuable are historical comparisons? In order to understand some of the changes we've seen and what it means to lead a global firm, I met with a number of current and former senior and managing partners of such firms. We talked about the past, and I also gained an insight into how they see the future.

Strategy, Leadership, Alignment and Management

Their view of the last 15 years can be summarised as the period in which four business concepts slowly evolved in legal practice. These are: the S-word (strategy), the L-word (leadership), the A-word (alignment—thank you McKinsey, Harvard) and the M-word (management). I found a high degree of congruence in these leaders' views on these four concepts. Konstantin Mettenheimer, joint senior partner of Freshfields, pointed to the liberalization of legal markets in the late 80s that opened the door for international legal practice. Duane Wall, former managing partner of White & Case, cited the consequent explosion in growth, which coincided with the start of globalization.

"Suddenly we had to build an executive team fit for the purpose: a team that could run the projects associated with international expansion (ultimately, outsourcing to India and insourcing to the Philippines); a team that could inspire lawyers and initiate action to achieve the required alignment of strategy, people, teams and processes," Wall said.

Mettenheimer told me: "During this period, Freshfields underwent a transformation from a collection of individuals to a more structured, more collaborative organization. Then, we went on to become a more classically managed firm." He explained: "To effect these changes, the secret was to ensure adequate consultation whilst establishing a clear sense of vision, uncompromising standards of performance, and individual accountability. We needed to create a collective sense of pride and direction, and recognise the importance of alignment. The Holy Grail was to develop a firm which was professional, partnerial and managed in equal measure."

Gary Senior, Managing Partner of Baker & McKenzie in London, added: "The whole concept of leadership has shifted. It wasn't even recognised 15 years ago. Neither was strategy. In the UK the professionalization of law firms started in the early 1990s. Since then, partners have moved their stance on leadership and management from reticence to recognition to acceptance to requirement! People now expect direction and guidance. Firms have gone from being unmanaged (and unmanageable) to being managed professionally."

To illustrate the importance and impact of leadership, and of assembling the right management team, Sir Nigel Knowles, Joint Chief Executive of DLA Piper, commented: "Take our business in the Middle

East. We started planning a presence in 2005 and within three years we had 130 lawyers and offices throughout the region. That kind of growth doesn't just happen. It takes strong leadership and courage. Global law firm leaders are now acting just like leaders in other spheres of commerce. There's been a coming of age in terms of law firm management."

Return on Collective Individuality

If the art of leadership is the achievement of strategic objectives through others, management is the effective implementation of action plans by those others. In this respect, law firms probably represent the ultimate challenge to senior and managing partners. So just how can they achieve the maximum return on collective individuality (ROCI)? Unsurprisingly, I also found some common ground in how these leaders describe their remit. What emerged were five strands that shape their working lives:

- Developing the vision and strategy

- Assembling the right management team and structure to ensure effective implementation of strategy and day-to-day operations

- Performing an internal pastoral role to inspire, support and motivate

- Ensuring a constant flow of effective communication

- Acting as external ambassador – the face of the firm

But what of the next 10-15 years? If strategy, leadership, organizational alignment and management had become so important, what was the scale of the challenge that lay ahead? Here, perspectives were more varied.

White & Case's Wall was clear in his view of the legal landscape: "Larger firms will get even larger, but still there will be no more than nine or ten global firms. The price of market entry at the global level is already too high. Beyond these firms, there will be more stratification of the legal market and consolidation will accelerate. In some jurisdictions there could be big opportunities for change with the advent of external investment and multi-disciplinary practices." In terms of practice, he said: "Commoditization will become a fact of life, but some firms will deal with it better than others."

The leadership team at Freshfields concurred. Ted Burke, Chief Executive, said in a recent press article: "Legal Process Outsourcing (LPO) will radically change the legal market. We will see more unbundling of the way legal services are currently delivered." His colleague, Mettenheimer, added: "Mechanised law will continue to be outsourced to low-cost jurisdictions. More complicated advice, however, will continue to be split between private practice and in-house counsel." He went on to predict: "Even for this complicated work, companies will increasingly buy an agreed volume of hours at an agreed fixed price." He continued: "The most complex, bet-the-ranch or highly-specialised work, however, will still be done by the best global practices. In-house counsel, meanwhile, will play a central role in managing the relationships with external legal advisers as well as taking on certain parts themselves rather than mandating firms."

Market Polarization

Mettenheimer agreed that concurrent with ongoing globalization there would be continued polarization of the market. But on the global stage he said: "The first firms to create truly integrated legal teams across the Americas, Europe and Asia will be the dominant firms. This is a lot easier said than done – I mean *truly* integrated." However, he did not see a rash of global MDPs (multi-disciplinary practices) being formed: "I doubt there will be mega mergers between accountants and lawyers," he said. "Global law firms will pursue strong client demand and productivity rather than a flags-on-map strategy."

In the light of the recent financial turmoil, Mettenheimer predicted that there would be more regulation (and more complexity of regulation) and added: "Like it or not, this will benefit lawyers, as long as it doesn't hurt the economy. Risk management will take its rightful place on the boards of many companies. However, it will be a different market, one in which de-leveraging will be the order of the day. It will be difficult for clients to invest money without debt and we will need to acclimatise to this."

One of the biggest challenges facing law firms is that clients will demand their lawyers finally become truly commercial in the way they think and operate. "Self-governance is an important part of partnership. But I would hope to see us taking advantage of the management skills and experience also available externally to help us run our business efficiently," said Mettenheimer.

Senior agreed, but added a note of caution: "Firms will structure themselves more like corporate businesses. They will become even more managed and organised, and in the UK the Legal Services Act will fuel these changes. But some international firms will face a challenge to become less imperial in leadership style. British and American senior and managing partners will no longer be able to dominate leadership roles. At Baker & McKenzie, we've had a succession of non-US leaders and we've learned that the different regions—Asia, Europe and the Middle East, the Americas—need to be properly represented at board level."

"The way I see it, the bi-polar world of New York and London has gone," added Knowles. "In future, the financial markets will operate in a more integrated, global way, taking account of other financial centres: Frankfurt, Dubai, Abu Dhabi, Mumbai, Hong Kong, Shanghai and Tokyo." He went on: "The long-term implications of the liquidity crisis are significant."

Senior believes that law firm leaders are still likely to be lawyers. "I don't see a whole spate of non-lawyer CEOs being appointed. However, the main lesson we can learn from other industries is the need to become much more comfortable in a global and multi-cultural environment," he said.

There was a slight divergence as to what else law firm leaders might learn from successful captains of industry. Senior was unequivocal in his view: "The most successful company CEOs recognise the importance of three things: appointing high calibre people to key positions around them; having the courage to do bold things; and fostering transparency."

According to Wall: "Corporations operate in a more command and control environment; law firms just aren't like that. You have to take people with you, somehow. What I can say, though, is that Jim Collins' book *Good to Great* is required reading for all of us." Knowles agreed: "Corporations could learn a lot from successful law firms about alignment."

Inspiring Confidence and Sustaining Momentum

The importance of "putting the right people in the right senior roles" was recognised by Mettenheimer: "We should do all we can to learn about the complete tool-kit of management from successful organizations in other industries. We need to study how their leaders become the embodiment of corporate vision through sheer drive and personal engagement. And we need to discover how these people take personal responsibility for inspiring confidence and ensuring momentum."

It was a comment that reminded me of a conversation I once had on a Mediterranean beach with my father-in-law. A retired company chairman in the air travel industry, I asked him the secrets of his success. His answer was swift and deceptively simple: "Personal drive, sheer hard work and never allowing myself to become remote."

This brings me to the ultimate question: what are the hallmarks of exceptional leaders?

According to the leaders with whom I met, *courage* was top of the list.

"Leadership involves some degree of friction; you can't be loved by everyone, but you hope to be respected; it's not a popularity contest!" said Mettenheimer. "What is important is to establish the right environment in which people can collaborate freely across borders," added Wall.

The ability to instil a *strong sense of direction* came next. It is crucial to inspiring confidence and enthusiasm.

Paying attention to the world outside was the third attribute. Wall explained: "Leaders must be adept at observing what's happening in the market so that they can adapt to change, competition and opportunity. They'd better not be caught asleep at the switch!"

This augurs well because research into the traits of successful business leaders invariably cites the words vision, courage, consistency, listening, communication and energy. Indeed, the latest research by leadership consultancy Whitehead Mann finds that the dominant attributes of effective leaders today are:

- Vision
- Clarity, consistency and integrity of purpose
- Competitive strategies for sustainable success
- Effective development of management team for the future

• Inspiration and engagement of people

The Whitehead Mann report sums it up nicely: "The most important factor is vision, which is intuitive rather than something which can be formally learnt. It is this which endows leaders with the ability to provide direction to their employees and which enables them to create a company where people want to work. It is a rare ability—to manage the present and create the future. But if the CEO can pull this off, they can build a lasting legacy."

Knowles shared his admiration for Bill Gates and Jack Welch: "Both had an idea which they turned into a vision. And both had the courage to turn that vision into a world-dominant reality."

It seems then that, in spite of the new digital age, some things change very little: having a healthy appreciation of the past; putting the best team in place to manage the present; and, most importantly, creating a future to which people can aspire—this is still what it takes to be an exceptional leader. ●

Bright Ideas: Insights from Legal Luminaries

Author Profiles

DEREK BENTON

Derek Benton is Director of International Operations, responsible for Martindale-Hubbell operations outside the US. He joined Reed Elsevier, parent of the LexisNexis group, in 1982. At Martindale, Derek has been involved in setting up European-based sales, marketing, and product development teams as well as the *Counsel to Counsel* forum for in-house lawyers. He has been in direct contact with bar associations, professional organizations and law firms of every size, across the world, over the past 21 years. Having experienced law firm marketing in numerous jurisdictions, Derek has helped shape LexisNexis Martindale-Hubbell's (LNMH) publishing and services.

E. Leigh Dance (Editor's note): In 1999, Derek and I launched the first *Counsel to Counsel* forum in Europe, and since then the forums around the world have informed Derek's work and many developments at LNMH. Derek is a fantastic and consistently solid colleague. He is an exceptionally kind and courteous man, an accomplished marathon runner, and a globe trotter like no other.

PETER J. BESHAR

Since late 2004, Peter J. Beshar has served as the General Counsel of Marsh & McLennan Companies and was appointed an Executive Vice President of MMC in 2006. Prior to joining MMC, Peter was a litigation partner in the New York office of Gibson, Dunn & Crutcher and Co-Chair of the firm's Securities Litigation Group. He previously served as Assistant Attorney General in charge of the New York State Attorney General's Task Force on Illegal Guns and as Special Assistant to the Honorable Cyrus Vance in the peace negotiations over the former Yugoslavia. After graduating from Yale University and Harvard Law School, Peter clerked for the Honorable Vincent Broderick of the US District Court for the Southern District of New York. He is a member of the Council on Foreign Relations and a trustee of the Rye Country Day School.

    ELD: In 2006 Peter flew to Chicago to speak at an IBA Conference session I had organized, stepping in at the last minute for his deputy GC. Peter's words about Marsh & McLennan's experience since 2004 made us all understand the nightmare of a high-profile crisis as if we had been there. Since then I've followed and admired the activities of MMC's in-house legal team under Peter's excellent leadership.

JEFFREY CARR

Jeffrey Carr has extensive experience in the full range of commercial and corporate law counseling issues affecting a global business, as well as corporate governance, compliance and dispute resolution. In his role as head of legal for FMC Technologies, Jeffrey designed and implemented the ACES™ risk/reward law firm engagement model, the FMC Technologies Corporate Compliance Program, and 1° Law™ Program, the subject of his essay. The FMC Technologies Legal Team was featured in the *Corporate Legal Times* in 2004 and *Inside Counsel* in 2008 as one of the 10 most innovative law departments, and has also been recognized by the Association of Corporate Counsel and the General Counsel Roundtable for its cutting-edge legal delivery services ideas.

    ELD: Jeff's enthusiasm is contagious, and though he jokes that being passionate about changing corporate legal services delivery is crazy, Jeff's contributions have been practical and valuable. At FMC, he walks the talk. If you *really* want to be entertained by Jeff, ask him about Jimmy Buffett. Amazingly, Jeff can connect Buffett's lyrics directly to theories of global counselling.

BRUNO COVA

Bruno Cova is co-chair of the Milan office of Paul Hastings. With experience leading the legal functions of major global companies and advising on global expansion and corporate crisis, he focuses on complex cross-border transactions such as restructurings, acquisitions of distressed companies and assets or companies impacted by wrongdoing, and advises directors and senior managers of corporations facing crises with strong legal or regulatory elements. Previously, Bruno was General Counsel of the Exploration & Production Division of Eni SpA, Chief

Compliance Officer of the EBRD, and Group General Counsel of Fiat SpA. Immediately prior to joining Paul Hastings he was chief legal adviser to the Commissioner appointed by the Italian government to investigate Europe's largest financial fraud at Parmalat, and deal with the company's restructuring. In 2003, while he was its General Counsel, Fiat Group received the "European In-House Legal Team of the Year" Award, and in 2004 he received the "Legal Week Award" for his work for Parmalat.

ELD: Ever since Nino Cusimano kindly introduced us in 2003, I've wondered how Bruno exudes such expertise, integrity and professionalism without a hint of arrogance or grandstanding. Always taking time to help others, Bruno is a good person and a tremendously dedicated lawyer. There's a big Bruno Cova fan club across Europe and among global counsel who've been through crises. I am so very proud of the pieces that Bruno and I have co-authored for *The Wall St. Journal* and *Financial Times*.

E. LEIGH DANCE

As President of ELD International, Inc., Elizabeth Leigh Dance advises global law firms on international expansion and business development, assisting firm management with developing and executing competitive growth strategies internationally as well as improving the productivity and performance of international offices. She also advises global corporate law departments, through special projects and retreats, on structuring and managing to achieve better results for their companies. With LexisNexis Martindale-Hubbell she co-founded and organizes the international series *Counsel To Counsel*: A Forum on Best Practices in Corporate Legal Services. Since 2000 Leigh has moderated more than 75 roundtables of senior corporate counsel in more than 25 cities on all continents. Leigh developed and produced the *Global Counsellors College* with PLC and Howrey, and co-chaired four global compliance conferences in the US and Europe in 2007 and 2008. She developed and co-chaired the 2008 *Wake Up to the Future: How Global Corporate Legal Services Must Change* conference hosted by Eversheds and ACC in New York City. Leigh's consultancy began in 1993, following 12 years of work experience in international development and public policy in Washington, and in New York as Vice President of The Chase Manhattan Bank with strategic planning, product management and marketing management assignments in 13 countries, and as head of marketing for a US Midwest law firm. Leigh has an International MBA from Thunderbird and speaks English, French and Italian. www.eldinternational.com

ROSS FISHMAN

Ross Fishman is the CEO of Fishman Marketing, helping law firms in marketing planning, branding, differentiation, and the development of collateral materials like Web sites, advertising and brochures. Fishman Marketing has launched campaigns for over 60 firms worldwide, which have received the Legal Marketing Association's (LMA) grand prize, the Best of Show award five times, a peer-selected 1998 Lifetime Achievement Award, and one of *Inc.* magazine's ten national Marketing Masters awards. In 2007, Ross was one of four selected for induction into the LMA's inaugural Hall of Fame. Known for his educational and entertaining style, he has spoken at over 250 firm retreats and training programs on five continents. Ross was a commercial litigator before becoming Marketing Director at an international firm, and later as Marketing Partner at Coffield Ungaretti & Harris launched the profession's first Written Service Guarantee. He has been quoted from *The New York Times* to the *New Zealand Lawyer,* to "All Things Considered" on National Public Radio (NPR). www.fishmanmarketing.com

ELD: Early in my legal services career, Ross Fishman stood out as a really funny speaker with very smart things to say. Then I learned that he is a creative wiz and a seriously talented writer, with a unique ability to make seemingly mundane things *new.* Later we became consulting allies, and I've been lucky to work with Ross on some fantastic international projects and know Ross as the devoted family man, father of four remarkable children.

TIM S. GLASSETT

At Hilton's World Headquarters, Tim Glassett was responsible for day to day management of the company's global law department of 40 lawyers. Hilton Hotels Corporation is a leading global hospitality company, with more than 3,000 hotels in 74 countries and territories, and more than 135,000 team members worldwide. Before joining Hilton in 2001, Tim was Senior Vice President and General Counsel for Edison Enterprises, an energy services company, and managing legal officer at H. F. Ahmanson & Company and Home Savings of America. Tim has both an MBA and a J.D. from University of Utah. Among other voluntary activities, Tim currently serves as Secretary and General Counsel of Plasticos Foundation, a charity that performs plastic surgeries to correct birth defects for children in developing countries.

ELD: When Tim spoke on a panel of experts at the Global Counsellors College in France, the junior in-house lawyers were captivated by his sage insights and practical advice, not to mention his friendly California style. I've learned much about leadership from Tim; he gives a lot of responsibility and independence to his team, and is always there for quiet direction and support.

ANN LEE GIBSON

Dr. Ann Lee Gibson has helped law firms compete for and win nearly US$600 million in new business. As a consultant to North American law firms, she advises firms on projects and issues surrounding new business development. She consults with firms and trains and coaches lawyers in the areas of high-stakes competitions, sales presentations, and competitive intelligence. She also works with firms that want to grow strategically by helping them develop competitive intelligence and proposal systems. Earlier in her career, she was Head of Marketing for the Nossaman firm and Gibson Dunn & Crutcher. Ann has published dozens of articles in many national publications, and speaks regularly at national and international conferences and law firm retreats. In 2006 she was inducted as a Fellow into the College of Law Practice Management. www.annleegibson.com

ELD: Ann is a breath of fresh air. She is a remarkable combination of warm southern style, intense powers of concentration, eagerness to learn, and a razor-sharp ability to point out what my father would prefer that I call "baloney." Ann is one of my consulting allies, and I benefit from her joyful sharing of original and astute observations and her very thoughtful analysis.

Author Profiles

FADI HAMMADEH

Fadi Hammadeh has over 15 years of regional and international experience as an in-house and private practice lawyer. He is head of legal of Dubai Properties Group, a multi-billion dollar Government-owned conglomerate which is developing mega projects in Dubai such as the Jumeirah Beach Residences, Business Bay and The Villa. Fadi has been involved in structuring, negotiating, and overseeing the execution of real estate, acquisition and development transactions inside and outside the UAE. He is responsible for developing a viable risk management policy for Dubai Properties Group and its businesses including retail, property & asset management, hospitality, project management and security. Fadi was previously General Counsel of the Land Company of the Dubai International Financial Centre (DIFC), legal advisor to the Majid Al Futtaim Group, and was an arbitration lawyer in the Paris office of Freshfields. He holds a Trium Executive MBA from London School of Economics, NYU and HEC in Paris, and three LLMs, one from University of London and two from the University of Paris 1—Assas and Sorbonne.

ELD: Fadi Hammadeh represents the best of the breed of talented senior corporate counsel coming from recently emerged markets. He has an exceptional blend of international business acumen and legal expertise, and is continually eager to learn ways that he can bring greater value as a lawyer and as a businessman. It is a delight to work with Fadi.

ALAN JENKINS

Alan chairs the Board of Eversheds and has been responsible for Eversheds' International strategic development, playing a central role in the firm's global expansion. He was formerly managing partner of Frere Cholmeley Bischoff, before its merger with Eversheds. As a lawyer, Alan practised in the fields of commercial litigation, international arbitration and professional negligence, and worked on many high profile cases. He has dealt with various government agencies and state-owned bodies around the world. Alan is Vice Chairman of the boards of trustees of the International Institute for Environment and Development and of the Foundation for International Environmental Law and Development. He is also a trustee of GAP Activity Projects Ltd.

ELD: Alan Jenkins is a global pioneer. He has impressed me with his achievements in carrying Eversheds' torch around the world, steadily guiding the firm through well-selected affiliations and mergers that have made it truly international today. Alan is a voice of continuity and yet he is always open and willing to consider and incorporate new ideas.

PETER KALIS

Peter Kalis' award-winning law practice has involved strategic advice to many of the nation's largest corporations. He has worked extensively with chief executive officers, boards of directors, and general counsel in the development and execution of proactive or defensive litigation strategies and strategies to preserve and access corporate insurance programs in response to a variety of novel and substantial claims. For his role as law firm K&L Gates' Chairman and Global Managing Partner, *The Lawyer* recently named Peter among the ten individuals in the global profession who will shape the international market for legal services in the next decade. Peter is a member of the American Law Institute and has served on Task Forces of the American Bar Association. He routinely addresses professional congregations on both practice and law firm leadership topics. Peter currently serves and has served on the board of many professional and non-profit organizations. He has a J.D. from Yale Law School, where he was Editor-in-Chief of *Yale Law Journal*. Peter was also a Rhodes Scholar in Philosophy at Oxford University.

ELD: One of my best consulting assignments ever was working with Peter Kalis on K&L Gates' first international expansion effort—to find a merger partner in the UK. Besides being a brilliant lawyer, Peter is a gentleman and a scholar. In this world of wavy principles, I greatly admire how solidly he holds his ground. We see Peter's impact as a global law firm leader and an independent thinker. One rises to every challenge when working with him, and feels lucky to do so.

DESPINA KARTSON

Despina Kartson, based in the firm's New York office, leads Latham & Watkins' global business development and marketing strategies across 28 offices spanning the United States, Europe, Asia, and the Middle East.

She oversees an 80+-strong business development department. Before joining Latham & Watkins in 2004, Despina worked for two decades both inside law firms and in the professional services industry. She was Vice President of Business Development at Bowne Business Solutions, a provider of outsourcing services to services industries and has worked for global law firms in senior technology positions, including at Cravath, Swain & Moore and White & Case LLP. Despina was the Marketing Partner Forum Co-chair in 2007 and 2008, and is 2009 President of the Metropolitan New York Chapter of the Legal Marketing Association. She has many national and local speaking engagements and as an author has published two books, *Computerized Litigation Support* and *Designing Litigation Support Databases* (John Wiley & Sons), and numerous articles. Despina serves on the Board of Advisors of the Women's Venture Fund (which identifies and works with emerging women entrepreneurs from distressed economic communities).

ELD: I think of Latham & Watkins' global expansion as the 'gold standard.' After seeing the firm's rapid and high quality growth over the last few years, it has been a pleasure to get to know Latham's business development leader. Despina is competence personified. She knows how to manage both structure and process in a multi-office global organization, and how to motivate a truly high-caliber international team.

BRUCE MacEWEN

A lawyer and consultant to law firms, Bruce MacEwen founded and publishes "Adam Smith, Esq." (www.AdamSmithEsq.com), which generates a third of a million page views per month, providing insights on the business of large, sophisticated law firms. Since the site's launch in late 2003, Bruce has published nearly 1,000 articles on "Adam Smith, Esq." on the economics of law firms, covering such topics as strategy, leadership, globalization, M&A, finance, compensation, cultural considerations and partnership structures. Bruce's consulting practice focuses on US, UK, and Canadian firms, with recent engagements such as developing strategic plans for departments, practice groups, and firms as a whole; pre-merger due diligence and post-merger integration; and improving associate recruitment and retention. Bruce has been CEO of a dot-com, was an in-house counsel in securities with Morgan Stanley/Dean Witter, and practiced litigation and corporate law with Shea & Gould and Breed, Abbott & Morgan in New York.

ELD: I am also of Scottish heritage and raised Presbyterian, so I can't speak objectively about Bruce MacEwen. But there's no need—if he were alive, even Adam Smith would likely join the applause for Bruce's superb blog. Bruce maintains uniquely high standards for the content and the message of *every* sentence he writes, week after week. What comes across in his posts (in addition to his unabashed love of economics) is Bruce's delightful, generous personality.

CHRIS MARSHALL

Chris Marshall manages and develops Reed Smith's pro bono, community and charity programmes for its Europe and Middle East offices. He works closely with the firm's clients, community and business partners on new initiatives both locally and internationally. Chris also chairs the Board of Trustees of Advocates for International Development (A4ID), an international lawyers' organization that harnesses legal skills to support pro bono to meet the UN Millennium Development Goals. A4ID connects lawyers with organizations that have a legal need, and also operates an education programme for lawyers and development professionals. Over the last two years A4ID has brokered over 200 projects across Africa, Asia and Latin America. Chris is a member of the UK Attorney General's International Pro Bono Committee. He and the team at A4ID won *The Lawyer* Pro Bono Team of the Year 2007 and for this work Reed Smith was also recognised by *Legal Business* as Corporate Social Responsibility Law Firm of the Year 2008.

ELD: Chris Marshall's vision for international pro bono, evidenced through his achievements with Reed Smith and with A4ID, are so impressive. Having started my career in international development, I have been thrilled to learn from Chris about A4ID's approach. A4ID connects many diverse dots to make free legal assistance more widely available around the world in situations where it is greatly needed.

DEBORAH MCMURRAY

Deborah is CEO and Strategy Architect of Content Pilot. As a consultant, she advises law firms on initiatives that focus a firm's strategy and its marketing investments. Deborah McMurray and her creative team develop targeted positioning and branding strategies for firms, including the creation of Web sites and Web-based proposal centers, collateral, advertising campaigns and other media. She is strategy architect and team leader for these projects, overseeing the Content Pilot LLC creative and development team. Deborah is an authority on the design and development of top law firm Web sites and an industry leader in law firm marketing metrics, helping firms measure and track return on investment. In 2008 Deborah was inducted into the LMA Hall of Fame, and in 2007 as a Fellow in the College of Law Practice Management. She is a co-author of the ABA's book, *Lawyer's Guide to Marketing on the Internet* (2nd and 3rd edition) and co-editor of *Lawyer's Guide to Marketing your Practice* (2nd ed.). Deborah's professional services career spans 24 years. From 1987-1998 she was marketing director of Texas-based Johnson & Swanson/Gibbs and Hughes & Luce, LLP.

ELD: As my trusted consulting ally, fellow moderator of LNMH's *Counsel To Counsel* sessions and collaborator on the *ELD Law Firm Directory Guides*, I've had many occasions to see Deborah's skills and *savoir faire*. She is an expert at what she does, and continually meets the highest of expectations with her superb project management skills. As Deborah's colleagues will unanimously tell you, she is a steadfast supporter and a loyal friend.

MARY MULLALLY

Mary qualified as a solicitor at Lewis Silkin in 1989. In 1990 she joined Alan Edwards, a niche housing and legal aid practice in Notting Hill Gate, where she was subsequently made a partner. In 1998 she joined Global Professional Media as the in-house correspondent for *Legal Week*. From 2001 to 2004 Mary edited *Legal Director*, a sister title to *Legal Week* which focused on management issues for in-house counsel. In 2004 Mary joined the Practical Law Company (PLC), a leading provider of legal know-how, transactional analysis and market intelligence for business lawyers. Mary is currently Head of Networks for Practical Law Company.

ELD: It's a good thing that not all qualified lawyers make a lifelong career in the practice. Corporate counsel in the UK and internationally (and consultants like me) have greatly benefitted from Mary Mullally's decision more than ten years ago to become a journalist and editor. I have huge respect for her work.

MICHAEL O'NEILL

Michael O'Neill has worldwide oversight for the Lenovo's legal, corporate governance, security and government relations activities. Prior to joining Lenovo, Michael was a partner at Howrey LLP, where he led the firm's international business and opened its Brussels office. Michael worked at Honeywell for 16 years in a variety of roles, culminating as VP and General Counsel (GC) for Transportation and Power Systems. He served as VP and GC for Europe, Middle East and Africa, and had earlier Honeywell roles as VP and Associate GC for Corporate and Human Resources and Assistant GC for Government Business and Technology Centers. In addition to his legal roles, for 10 years he was VP of Global Contract Management at Honeywell. Michael also has served as in-house counsel at Westinghouse at the Defense & Electronics Center. He holds a J.D. and an MBA from the University of Baltimore, and a Master in Government Contracting from George Washington University. Michael has served on various boards, most recently that of TRW International.

ELD: Michael is a very intelligent lawyer and caring counsellor with a huge capacity for fun and games. When Mike, Mary K Young and I produced the Global Counsellors College, he had an uncanny ability to mix complex legal issues, a super network of global counsel, rock music and ping pong. It made for a phenomenal program that got rave reviews. Mike has many great stories, but beware if you get him started...

NORM RUBENSTEIN

A Zeughauser Group partner, Norm Rubenstein is widely regarded as one of the legal industry's most experienced and innovative marketing and positioning strategists. As the chief marketing officer of three global law firms and as a consultant to numerous others, Norm has collaborated with law firm leadership on strategy designed to increase client and market share, on award-winning branding initiatives, and on the evaluation of their marketing organizations and investments. For his work at Orrick, Norm was honored with the Spherion Marketing Director of the Year Award. In 2007 he was among four inaugural honorees of the LMA Hall of Fame. Norm's consulting practice reflects a decade as an in-house legal marketer; ten years as director of publishing and marketing of Edison Electric Institute, one of the nation's largest trade associations; and five years as a teacher at the University of Virginia (UVA). Norm has served as national president of LMA as well as president of its Mid-Atlantic Chapter. He holds B.A. and M.A. degrees from Tulane University, and completed his doctoral course work at UVA.

ELD: This is not the first time I've revealed that Norm is my long lost brother, separated from me at birth. It's not true, but it feels that way—though I could never match Norm's eloquent English, sophisticated wit or couture wardrobe. For more than 15 years we've had rewarding experiences working together at McKenna, at Orrick, and as consultants. What stands out is Norm's true kindness. He has been extravagantly generous with me, both personally and professionally.

JOLENE OVERBECK

Jolene Overbeck currently serves as the Chief Marketing Officer of DLA Piper, the world's largest law firm. She oversees the firm's marketing and business development activities throughout the US, coordinating with the firm's offices in Asia, Europe, and the UK. She is responsible for brand, strategic communications, business development, practice and sector marketing and marketing technology systems. Jolene has nearly 30 years experience in legal marketing and is one of the industry's most experienced and well-regarded marketing professionals. Prior to joining DLA Piper, she served as CMO at Latham & Watkins for more than 12 years, and shaped its marketing program. She subsequently joined Shearman & Sterling in New York, and spent two years restructuring and refocusing the marketing and business development program. Prior to joining DLA Piper, Jolene was a partner with the Zeughauser Group, a leading strategic law firm consultancy. She began her career with Orrick where she was that firm's first marketing director.

ELD: I have always learned from Jolene when we've shared the podium at conferences over the years, and I had the good fortune to work on a project with Jolene and her team at Shearman & Sterling. She is a superb manager and an exceptional team player, she's fun to be with, and there is no one that knows law firm marketing better.

THOMAS J. SABATINO, Jr.

Thomas J. Sabatino Jr. is Executive Vice President and General Counsel of Schering-Plough Corporation. He oversees the legal operations of the company, including formulating corporate legal policy and supervising inside and outside counsel and directing corporate activities pertaining to corporate communications, federal legislation, government relations and corporate security. Tom joined Schering-Plough in his present position in April 2004. He most recently served as Senior Vice President and General Counsel for Baxter International Inc. in Deerfield, Ill. Tom was named General Counsel of Baxter International in 1997 and added the title Senior Vice President in 2001. He has also worked for law firms in both Chicago and Boston during his career. Tom has a J.D. from University of Pennsylvania Law School and is a member of the Bar in California, Illinois and Massachusetts.

ELD: I hadn't known Tom for long when he got stuck in my office elevator in Rome, along with a Barclays in-house lawyer and Fred Krebs of ACC. Luckily they got out quickly, and it didn't phase Tom—he was happy to be in *'la citta eterna,'* and he's a guy that rolls with the punches. Tom is a team player, a consummate professional, and a very intelligent, highly regarded General Counsel. It is always a pleasure to work with him.

HELENA SAMAHA

Helena is a corporate lawyer with more than 15 years in diverse transactional experience in banking & finance, M&A and joint ventures, and commercial relationships such as franchising, supply and distribution across Europe, US, Middle East and Africa. Her experience spans the telecommunications & media, leisure, transport, pharmaceutical and financial sectors. Helena is currently the Paris-based General Counsel – Europe, Middle East, Africa for AlixPartners, a US-headquartered global performance improvement, corporate turnaround and financial advisory services firm. Prior to joining AlixPartners, Helena was a partner in London with DLA Piper, in the Technology, Media & Commercial group, where she took the lead in developing an international platform for serving day-to-day legal needs of global clients. Previously for seven years Helena was Group Legal Director for the Virgin Group and was involved in numerous innovative corporate transactions globally. She started her career at Clifford Chance. Helena holds an LLM from Kings College London, and a "Maitrise de Droit" Assas-Pantheon in Paris.

ELD: Helena Samaha exemplifies the truly global lawyer, bridging global law firms and global corporate law departments. Born in Lebanon, she went to high school partly in Beverly Hills, college in Aix-en-Provence and law school in Paris and London. Helena's law firm convergence effort while at Virgin is still regarded as best practice. I truly admire Helena's distinguished, intelligent and human approach.

SIMON SLATER

Having spent 10 years in the sales school of hard knocks with SmithKline Beecham (now gsk) and Pfizer, and a fascinating spell in business-to-business brand management with Swedish multinational, SCA, Simon became one of the early pioneers of professional service firm management in 1989. Over the next 15 years he worked in marketing and general management with the boards of leading practices - DTZ Group plc, Charles Russell LLP, Eversheds LLP and Taylor Wessing LLP. During this time he developed a reputation for bringing a refreshingly pragmatic approach to the leadership and management of professional firms, be they publicly quoted or private partnership. As Managing Director of First Counsel Consulting Limited, Simon now provides strategic advice, close counsel and practical support to law firm leaders in their quest for sustained growth. He also serves as non executive director of a number of organizations outside the legal market.

ELD: Simon has a voracious appetite for law firm strategy and global legal industry issues, and for years we communicated by email and phone, posing questions and sharing ideas, before we finally met in person. Interactions with Simon are always fun and intellectually stimulating; I admire his experience and tremendous energy.

ADAM SMITH

Adam Smith is the General Counsel of EADS Defence & Security, a division of EADS with sales of €5.5bn, where he leads a team of around 80 people. Prior to this, he worked in EADS Paris headquarters for ten years, running the Mergers & Acquisitions legal department. Adam started his career at Lovells in London as an insolvency lawyer. In a quest to see whether there is more to life than just law, he has also tried his hand at architecture and investment banking, but now realizes that law is indeed all there is. Adam holds an LLB from University College London and an MBA from London Business School. He is a Solicitor of England and Wales. A British and French national, Adam now lives in Munich, where at least the beer is better than in Paris.

ELD: Is it his confidence as a talented in-house lawyer that gives Adam the courage to write with such humor? We have to put up with a fair share of big lawyer posturing in global business, but Adam Smith never takes himself or anyone else too seriously. I was thrilled when he agreed to write an essay, and puzzled by his topic choice. Then I laughed right through his draft. As with all comedy, there is always much truth in Adam's words.

PAUL SMITH

Paul is an Eversheds Partner, an elected member of the firm's Board of Directors, and Chair of its Regulatory practice. An environmental lawyer and litigator, Paul has defended many multinationals in relation to criminal investigations in the UK, Europe and North America. The investigations have ranged from chemical plant explosions, insider dealing, railway disasters and price-fixing to environmental incidents. Additionally, Paul is a recognized expert on law firm partnering and convergence. He consults with many global corporate law departments on their structures, processes and practices to derive greater value from outside counsel. Paul is part of the Eversheds team involved in the Tyco convergence project in Europe, Middle East and Africa, where Tyco used its innovative 'SMARTER' model to consolidate its hundreds of law firms across 37 jurisdictions to one: Eversheds. In 2008, *Legal Business* honored Paul Smith as 'Lawyer of the Year', one of the most prestigious awards in the UK, for his contributions to global client relationship management.

ELD: Few law firms are doing much truly *new* in managing global client relationships, and Eversheds is one of the exceptions. Paul and I have known each other for 12 years and worked together for six. With his positive vision, affable style, smarts and stamina, Paul has driven significant change within the firm and for the benefit of its clients. In interviewing Paul, I tried to get him to tell his story, so that readers could learn from this very talented innovator.

JOHN H. STOUT

John Stout is an officer and shareholder of Fredrikson & Byron, practicing principally in business organization, finance and governance. John represents family-owned, closely-held and publicly-owned businesses both domestically and internationally. He advises executives, boards, board committees, directors and officers on governance, risk assessment, legal compliance, and protection against liability. John has served as an expert witness on corporate governance matters, and frequently writes and speaks on governance subjects. He is an Adjunct Professor at the University of St. Thomas Law School, teaching corporate governance, and a past director of the National Association of Corporate Directors. John is a Vice Chair of the American Bar Association Corporate Governance Committee, and co-chairs ABA subcommittees on International Governance Developments and Nonprofit Governance. He also serves on the Boards of several nonprofit and for-profit corporations.

ELD: He was practicing mostly entertainment and securities law when we met, and on the night before my first job interview, my would-be boss (John) and his wife took me to hear his client, Prince, give a rare performance at Glam Slam, a local Minneapolis club that John represented. That's just typical John: eclectic and excellent. He never stops learning and branching out with his highly successful practice, and is now among the top governance lawyers globally.

DAVID SYED

David Syed, a partner in Orrick's Paris office, is the senior partner for Europe and a member of the global firm's Executive Committee. A member of the firm's European Finance Group, his practice focuses on complex financings and significant restructurings. He also has extensive experience in international contracts, corporate transactions, and cross-border transactions. Before joining Orrick, David was a partner with Watson, Farley & Williams from 1992 to 2002. He spent four years as an in-house lawyer in international contracts at Renault in Paris, followed by two years as an associate and partner at Baker & McKenzie in Paris. David has an

LL.B. from Universite' de Reims and an LL.M. from University of Exeter.

ELD: In global legal services our paths cross with others travelling in the same circles. I am always looking out for big thinkers and change makers, and years ago I found both in David Syed. In the interview for this book, the two of us had a blast imagining out loud our vision of tomorrow's great global law firm. David is an impact player, and Orrick is lucky to have him.

MARY K YOUNG

Mary K Young is one of the only legal industry marketing experts who brings a demonstrated track record of corporate branding success to her work developing and implementing marketing programs for law firms. Mary K established her reputation as a legal marketing innovator during her tenure as CMO of Howrey LLP from 2000-2006. Partnering with firm leadership, she developed and launched new positioning and advertising for the firm and a new corporate identity, was instrumental in the firm's strategic planning initiatives and the integration of a major merger partner. Between 2001 and 2004, Mark K developed and implemented marketing plans for Howrey's new presences in London, Brussels, Amsterdam, and Paris. Earlier in her career, Mary K was with Kraft Foods, where she was Category Business Director for Kraft Singles, leading a team of 50, with marketing and profit and loss responsibility for the $870 million revenue business. She also served as Senior Vice President of the Distilled Spirits Council of the US. Mary K holds an M.B.A. in Marketing from UCLA.

ELD: Consultants don't get many projects as fulfilling as those I had in working with Mary K for five years on Howrey's expansion in Europe. Mary K's executive experience, confidence and skills made her a great client, and also enabled her to make a major impact on the firm's strategy and direction. We worked hard and had lots of laughs—she is a pro, through and through.

Index

For more information

and to contact the editor

or essay authors, go to

www.BrightIdeasGlobalLaw.com